Young Readers Nature Library
THE EARTH

Young Readers Nature Library
Adapted from the LIFE Nature Library

THE EARTH

Arthur Beiser
and the Editors of TIME-LIFE BOOKS

TIME-LIFE BOOKS, ALEXANDRIA, VIRGINIA

ON THE COVER: A volcano in
action, Mexico's Paricutín
sends colored arcs of flaming
rock high into the air. The volcano
may spew over 2,000 tons of
material a minute.

Other Publications:
THE SEAFARERS
THE ENCYCLOPEDIA OF COLLECTIBLES
THE GREAT CITIES
WORLD WAR II
HOME REPAIR AND IMPROVEMENT
THE WORLD'S WILD PLACES
THE TIME-LIFE LIBRARY OF BOATING
HUMAN BEHAVIOR
THE ART OF SEWING
THE OLD WEST
THE EMERGENCE OF MAN
THE AMERICAN WILDERNESS
THE TIME-LIFE ENCYCLOPEDIA OF GARDENING
LIFE LIBRARY OF PHOTOGRAPHY
THIS FABULOUS CENTURY
FOODS OF THE WORLD
TIME-LIFE LIBRARY OF AMERICA
TIME-LIFE LIBRARY OF ART
GREAT AGES OF MAN
LIFE SCIENCE LIBRARY
THE LIFE HISTORY OF THE UNITED STATES
TIME READING PROGRAM
LIFE NATURE LIBRARY
LIFE WORLD LIBRARY
FAMILY LIBRARY:
  HOW THINGS WORK IN YOUR HOME
  THE TIME-LIFE BOOK OF THE FAMILY CAR
  THE TIME-LIFE FAMILY LEGAL GUIDE
  THE TIME-LIFE BOOK OF FAMILY FINANCE

Contents

1
A Small but
Very Special Planet   7

2
Cloudy Beginnings
of the Earth   25

3
The Mighty Engine
of the Atmosphere   43

4
Erosion: Forces
That Shape the Land   63

5
The Ever-moving
Ground beneath Us   79

6
A Record of Life
in the Rocks   99

7
The Uncertain Future
of the Earth   113

Index   126
For Further Reading   128
Credits and Acknowledgments 128

1

A Small but Very Special Planet

This is a journey to the earth. The trip begins far out in the universe, within a cluster of galaxies that are huddled together in what astronomers call a Local Group. One member of this cosmic family, itself made up of perhaps 250 billion stars, has a graceful pinwheel-like form. This is the Milky Way. As galaxies go it is only of medium size, yet its dimensions are hard for the mind to grasp. From one edge to the other it measures some 100,000 light-years. Its central bulge is as much as 15,000 light-years thick. And one light-year—the distance that light travels in a year at the speed of 186,282 miles a second—is just less than six thousand billion miles.

Two thirds of the way from the center of the Milky Way, where the stars begin to thin out, there shines an ordinary, yellowish star. It has plenty of room in which to move around, for its nearest neighbors in the galaxy lie four light-years—24 trillion miles—away. This lonely star, which glows from afar as weakly as a firefly, is our sun. Among its own family of faithfully circling planets, satellites, asteroids, meteoroids and comets, one oddly matched pair

THE BLUE PACIFIC, dotted with clouds that seem to float on its surface, stretches to a far-distant horizon in this picture taken by an astronaut soaring at an altitude of 100 miles. Beyond, the deep blackness of space outlines the curve of the earth, which is clearly noticeable at this height.

Strange Ideas about the World

BABYLONIANS, who lived around 3000 B.C., believed that the earth was a hollow mountain supported and surrounded by the sea. Inside this mountain lay the dark world of the dead. Across the curve of the sky moved the sun, moon and stars.

EGYPTIANS saw the earth as a resting god and the heavens as a gracefully bent goddess. Between them sat the god of the atmosphere, supporting the skies. The sun god, shown in his boat, sailed each day across the heavens into the death of night.

is the earth and its companion, the moon.

A minor planet bound to an ordinary star in the outskirts of one galaxy among billions—this is the earth. Approached in this way, from the chill reaches of infinite space, it would be all too easy to miss—a speck almost beneath notice except for one thing: of all the places that might possibly support human life, the earth is the only place we know of that does. Its interior and its "skin," its atmosphere, its climate and even its behavior in space, form an environment in which life flourishes.

Long before men had any real understanding of the shape or size of their planet,

of its humble place in the universe, they felt in their bones that each native valley, sheltered harbor or game-rich plain they lived in was somehow central to the entire cosmic scheme of things. In ancient Greece, all the gods of the universe were thought to dwell on a medium-sized mountain, Olympus, 150 miles from Athens. China, although torn and occupied again and again by barbarians, has always held firmly to the proud little title of "Central Nation." Not many decades ago, Boston's claim to be the "Hub of the Universe" was no joke among many Bostonians. Behind each of these and many similar sentiments lay a certain logic; after

8

HINDUS in India had many ideas about the earth. Some thought it was held up by elephants, which caused earthquakes when they moved. The elephants stood on a turtle representing the god Vishnu, which rested on a cobra, the symbol of water.

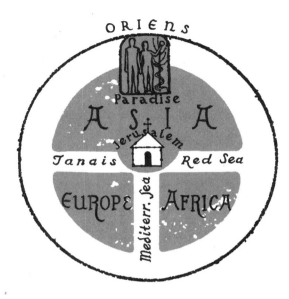

CHRISTIANS of the Middle Ages based their ideas on religious views. They divided the earth into three continents, with Jerusalem at the center and the Garden of Eden in Asia. The word Tanais stands for the Don River, an important trade route then.

all, any man is the center of his own circular horizon; any kingdom is the center of surrounding kingdoms; to man the earth is the center of the universe. It was a long time before anyone really thought about the size of the planet itself.

Though earlier philosophers had concluded that the earth was a globe, it was not until about 250 B.C. that an Alexandrian Greek, Eratosthenes, used geometry on the problem of the earth's total dimension. In Syene, an Egyptian town some 5,000 stadia (500 miles) south of Alexandria, there was a deep, dry well. Eratosthenes learned that at noon on the longest day of the year the sun's light shone directly down the well shaft. In Alexandria on that same day, he knew, the noon sun was not vertical, but cast a slight shadow. Eratosthenes used a simple geometric calculation to show that the difference in angle between Syene and Alexandria was about one fiftieth of a circle. So, 5,000 stadia multiplied by 50 gave Eratosthenes the first close estimate of the earth's circumference that we know about. Translating from stadia to miles, his amazingly accurate measurement comes out to 25,000 miles for circumference (the modern measure at the equator is 24,902) and 8,000

miles for the earth's diameter (the modern mean is 7,917 miles).

For such rough measurement, Eratosthenes' achievement was remarkable, but was somehow ignored or lost. Thus it was that Christopher Columbus, 1,700 years later, set off westward around the world to reach the Indies with a far smaller earth in mind. Despite what folklore says, Columbus knew —as did any other master mariner of his day —that the earth was a sphere; what he did not know was the earth's true size.

Today, thanks especially to measurements that were made during the International Geophysical Year (1957-1958), we know exactly what the earth's dimensions are. Indeed, long before the IGY men were aware that the earth was not a perfect sphere. Even before this fact was demonstrated by measurement, Isaac Newton had predicted it. Field work in the 18th Century confirmed Newton's prediction—

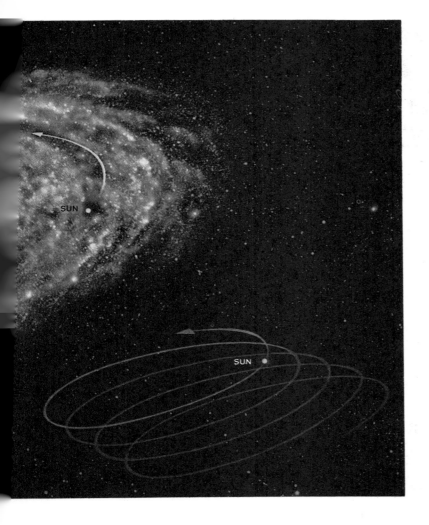

Spiraling into Space

As the earth and the other planets orbit around the sun, the sun itself moves through space at 150 miles per second (*small arrow, left*), swinging around with the other stars of the Milky Way in its own kind of orbit once every 200 million years. At the same time the whole Milky Way is plunging along through space (*large arrow*). The two motions together make the sun and its family of planets trace a spiral path (*lower right*).

at the equator the earth is 26.7 miles thicker than it is when measured from Pole to Pole. Even more exact measurements, based on the movements of America's IGY Vanguard I satellite, have shown that the highest points of the equatorial bulge (a matter of 25 feet) lie a little to the south of the earth's equatorial midline.

For most purposes though, the earth might as well be round. If all our planet's dimensions were shrunk to a globe about five feet across, the human eye would not be able to detect the difference—about a fifth of an inch—between the diameters at the equator and at the Poles. A fine coat of paint would be thicker than the continents' average height above sea level, and a light pinprick would probe this model earth's crust more deeply than man's deepest oil wells have reached into our planet.

If and when a space colony is established, perhaps halfway between the earth and the

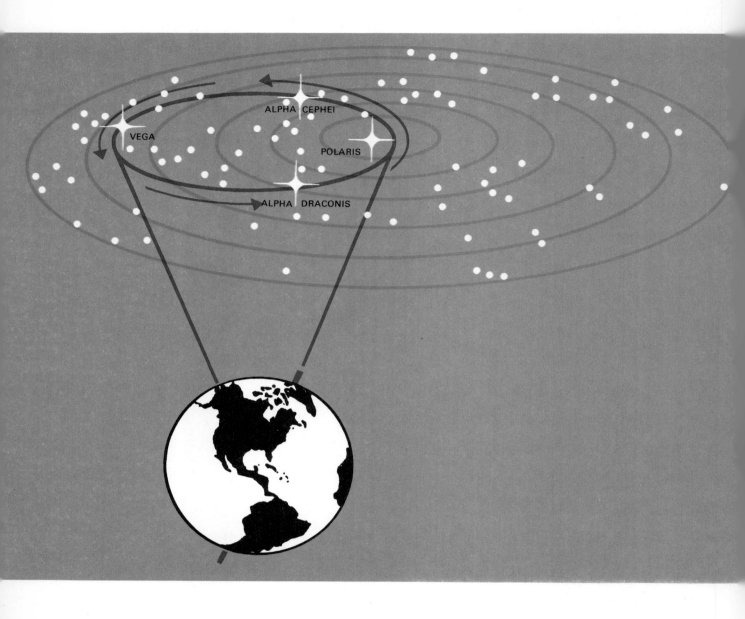

A Slowly Wobbling Earth

Over a period of 22,000 years, the axis of the earth shifts, describing a complete circle like the slowly weaving head of a spinning top. Today the axis points to Polaris, which we use as our "North Star." By the year 7500 A.D., it will point to Alpha Cephei; by 14,000 A.D., to Vega. Then it will swing around to Alpha Draconis—which was the North Star 5,000 years ago—before returning to point once again to Polaris.

moon, human beings will get such a scaled-down view of their planet. Already, astronauts on their way to and from the moon have seen that the earth is a colorful, ever-changing globe. Its sunlit face is bluish and its clouds, which are conspicuous, are often arrayed in long lines with clear gaps between them. As photographs have already shown us, the land masses of the earth can be distinguished from the oceans by their color. The land areas appear to be a delicate red-brown; the water varies from a light blue-green to deep blue. A dazzling splash of light marks the sun's reflection on the surface of any body of water.

A space colonist could easily follow the progress of large events on the earth from a distance of 115,000 miles or so. The annual cycle of vegetation would be reflected in color changes on the continents, and it might even be possible to trace the seasonal advance and retreat of the snow cover in the high latitudes of the Northern Hemisphere. By keeping track of the drift of clouds across the surface, an observer could follow both the westward flow of the trade winds and the eastward procession of the major weather systems in the earth's middle latitudes.

Certain other phenomena on earth would be harder to detect. A sensitive radio receiver, however, would reveal that at least a portion of man's multitude of radio signals penetrates the upper zones of the earth's atmosphere and passes on into space. A space observer would also be able to watch the earth's daily rotation on its own axis. This is the motion that gives us day and night as each place on the earth faces toward and then away from the sun.

The earth also revolves around the sun in the period of time we call a year, a 600-million-mile sweep that takes almost exactly 365¼ days. This trip around the sun, combined with the earth's tilt, is the movement that is responsible for the seasons. The earth's axis, the imaginary line drawn through the earth between the North and South Poles, does not stand straight up and down in relation to the sun. If it did, the equator would always point directly toward the sun, and there would be no seasons, just perpetual summer at the equator and eternal winter at the poles.

But this is not the case. When it is winter in the Northern Hemisphere, the North Pole points away from the sun, and the South Pole points toward the sun. This is why the seasons north of the equator are the exact opposite of those in the south. The longest day of the Northern Hemisphere's year (and the beginning of the summer season) falls around June 22, which is the shortest day of the Southern Hemisphere's year and marks the beginning of its winter.

Yet another movement causes the earth's axis to point to different parts of the sky. This movement is very slight, and terribly difficult to detect. But it has one noticeable effect: over a period of thousands of years the axis points at one, then another, then

Clear and Cold

Because the earth's axis is tilted in relation to its path around the sun, the Northern and Southern Hemispheres do not receive equal amounts of sunshine at any given time. When the Northern Hemisphere is tipped away from the sun, the sun's rays strike it at a slant, producing less warmth. This brings winter to a place like New York (*black dot at right*), with snow and frosty scenery (*below*). At the same time, it is summer in the Southern Hemisphere.

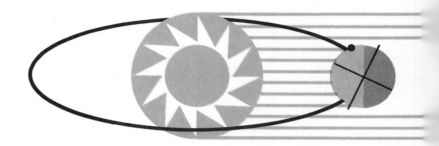

another star, and the star we call the North Star changes. The ancient Egyptians, living 5,000 years ago, had a different north star from the one we have today. Their north star, named Alpha Draconis, was in Draco constellation. Our north star, Polaris, is located in the Little Dipper. About 12,000 years from now the north star will be Vega, which is, conveniently, the brightest star in the northern sky. Even farther in the future, in the year 28,000 A.D., Polaris will again be the north star, and then the cycle will go on to repeat itself, as it has for hundreds of millions of years.

In addition to these movements, the earth shares two more motions with the other members of the solar system. In one of these, the earth follows the sun's own 12-mile-per-second journey through our local star cloud, traveling in the general direction of the constellation Hercules. In the other motion, the earth follows the sun in its major journey—a great, wheeling sweep around the hub of the Milky Way, a trip that takes 200 million years to complete.

Always close to the earth as it moves through space is its single satellite, the moon. We cannot study the earth's history as a planet without also studying this neigh-

14

Warm and Wet

When the Northern Hemisphere tips toward the sun, the sun's rays strike it more directly, producing higher temperatures. In addition, a given spot stays in the larger sunlit zone for a longer period of time as the earth rotates; on the day in late June that the axis tilts closest to the sun, New York (*dot*) gets a full 15 hours of daylight. The higher temperatures and increased hours of sunlight produce the welcome scenery of green forests.

bor, which is often thought of as a sister planet. Satellites of the outer planets are as big as or bigger than our moon—Jupiter's Ganymede is three times larger—but no other body in the sun's family has proportionally so large a companion as does the earth. The moon is not only very close to the earth but it has a diameter that is more than a quarter the size of the earth's and more than two thirds the size of Mercury's.

Furthermore, the rocks brought back from the moon are enough like those on earth to show that the two bodies were formed near each other in space. The moon may have circled the earth, even as it was taking

shape, or it may have been captured whole by the earth's gravity. It is also possible that the raw material for the moon was flung out from a liquid earth when the earth collided with another planetary body.

This lesser twin circles the earth in an elliptical orbit once each 27⅓ days. With each such revolution, the moon also rotates on its axis exactly once, so that the earth's inhabitants never see the "back" of the moon. Actually, the moon's axis is tilted, so that we glimpse both its north polar and south polar regions; in addition, its shape and motions are irregular enough that its swaying and nodding have permitted us to photograph

15

more than half—59 per cent—of the moon's total surface from the earth. Brilliantly lighted by the sun during the lunar day, the earthward face of the moon is dimly illuminated during the lunar night by sunlight that is reflected from the earth.

Despite the moon's similar origin, it is far different from the earth today. Its airless, waterless landscape is dramatically marked by vast dark plains (once thought by astronomers to be seas and hence named *ma-*

ria, a Latin word meaning "seas"). Its thousands of spectacular craters are as much as 180 miles across. Since the moon has no real atmosphere, and thus no rain or running water, the sort of erosion that continually wears down, rounds and softens the landscape here on the earth does not exist there. Its sharp-edged features are smoothed down only by dust from meteorite impacts, by particles transported from the sun on the solar wind, and by the extreme changes in tempera-

16

ture—from 200° F. to lower than −300° F.

What does the lunar landscape tell us about the earth's own past? Once it was believed that the craters on the moon represented a long series of volcanic eruptions such as the earth has often known. Today scientists still believe that some of the moon's craters were produced by volcanic action, and that these *maria* look relatively smooth now because their giant craters were

(Text continued on page 20)

"Earthshine" on the Moon

An artist's drawing of the moon's barren landscape shows a mammoth crater bathed in sunlight reflected from the earth, seen in the distance at right. A few years ago such illustrations, based on earthbound-telescope sightings, were the only views of what the moon's surface might be like. Since then space vehicles have taken close-up photographs *(next page)*.

Learning from the Moon

We may learn more about the history of our solar system from the moon than we can from the earth's surface, which is constantly changing. Most of the lunar surface today is very much as it was more than 2.5 billion years ago. Though meteorites continue to pock the moon, they are smaller than the one that made the mountain-studded Copernicus crater *(above)*. This crater—which is as large as Puerto Rico—appears by itself in the center of the picture opposite. Lunar topsoil, seen at right under a footpad of Surveyor I, consists of meteoritic rubble and powdery lava rock much like that found on earth.

filled with lava. But most of the craters—and most, if not all, of the *maria*—have been made by collisions with other bodies during the course of the moon's lifetime. Following this clue in recent years, we are now detecting the nearly vanished traces of similar, stupendous collisions on the earth. We are also studying the chunks, lumps, fragments and dust specks that continually rain down upon the earth from space.

Not long ago many people believed that the brief flashes in the night sky that we now know are meteor trails were somehow involved with the atmosphere and with the weather in general ("meteor," from which we get our word "meteorology," comes from the Greek for "high in the air"). There was logic in such a view; but it was based on the inaccurate assumption that lightning bolts produced something called "thunderstones" —which were actually peculiar rocks, or more often, the crude, unrecognized flint tools of early man.

Meteor flashes, too, were sometimes accompanied by thunderous sounds and unidentifiable fragments of stone or iron. Even with today's understanding, the matter of meteors still involves complex language. Specialists are very careful to distinguish between *meteoroids* (matter, regardless of size or composition, that drifts through space), *meteors* (the flashes of light produced by a meteoroid as it is heated glowing hot by its passage through the earth's atmosphere), and finally *meteorites* (the fragments, ranging from dust

20

Our Meteorite Relatives

The composition of meteorites, like that of the moon, gives us clues to the make-up of the earth, because they too were formed from matter in our solar system. The pock-marked chunk at the right is an iron-nickel meteorite that landed in Oregon in 1902. It is the largest ever recovered in this country and weighs 14 tons. The huge crater below, four fifths of a mile across and 600 feet deep, was made in Arizona in prehistoric times by a 15,000-ton meteorite that exploded and scattered into dust.

to huge rocks, that survive the fiery passage and reach the earth).

Meteorites are of three general classes: irons—composed 98 per cent or more of nickel-iron; stony irons—composed roughly half-and-half of nickel-iron and a kind of mineral known as olivine; and stones. Most of the meteorites that have so far been found belong to the last group. All meteorites offer useful clues to the history of the earth, for not only are they fellow members of the solar system, but they are probably as old as the earth itself.

During the earth's history spectacular meteor falls have brought irons weighing billions of tons smashing into the earth. But aside from these, a vast amount of meteoritic dust continually falls from the heavens. Estimates range from a few thousand to a few million tons every year. This dust consists of tiny particles ranging in size from a ten thousandth to a hundredth of an inch across. Meteoritic dust particles have been found around the world and because many of them contain iron, they can be extracted magnetically from rain water.

Many meteor showers occur in streams with established orbits. Some of these orbits are known to be the same as the orbits of former comets. Therefore, one might suppose that meteor showers represent the debris left in the wake of comets, past or present. But it is doubtful that such "comet-dust" meteoroids are ever large enough, by the time they reach the earth's surface, to be studied. The particles are so small that by the time they are burned in the atmosphere there is almost nothing left.

Most scientists feel that the meteoroids that do reach the earth as meteorites are fragments of asteroids; a belt of these objects orbits the sun between Mars and Jupiter. It is likely that many meteorites were once asteroid fragments that were knocked from their paths and into orbits that brought them within the field of the earth's gravitational pull. But whatever their source, the meteorites that have fallen and continue to fall to the earth—and onto the moon—not only offer tantalizing clues to the composition of those interior parts of our planet that lie beyond reach, but bring us clues to the earth's origin as well.

Two Billion Years of History

The mightiest gorge on any continent, the Grand Canyon reveals rock more than two billion years o where the Colorado River has cut 6,000 feet deep into arid plateau land. The river has been carving out the rocky valley for 10 million years, and will continue to do so for millions yet to come.

2

Cloudy Beginnings of the Earth

While man has long known about the earth's size and shape, his understanding of the planet's origin—and exactly what it is made of—is much less complete.

The earth certainly has not existed forever. If it had, radioactive elements still in its crust would have decayed into different, inactive elements long ago. The earth is old indeed—today most geologists accept a figure of at least 4.5 billion years—but once upon a time there was no earth, and how it was born presents one of the most fascinating riddles in science.

There has been no lack of attempted solutions. Some ancient mythologies pictured the young earth as a warm body of liquid. The philosopher Descartes in 1644 saw it as a sunlike, glowing body. Immanuel Kant and the Marquis de Laplace, in the 18th Century, thought it condensed out of a ga-

BILLOWING STEAM and an angry sky offer a vivid picture of what a young earth looked like billions of years ago, when volcanoes spewed rocks and vapor from a hot interior to a cooling surface. The rocks built up the land; the vapor provided clouds and water.

seous cloud surrounding the sun. Other hypotheses held that the earth was thrown out of a sun made unstable by its enormous rate of spin, or torn away from it by the force of a collision, or near-collision, with some passing star.

The whole question of the earth's evolution is, of course, linked to the larger questions of the origin of the solar system, of stars in general, of galaxies—and of the entire universe. Man tries to answer these questions with theories, but it is beyond his power to know exactly what happened.

With this warning, what can be said about the earth's first days? Many astronomers now agree that a chain of events probably started inside a huge cloud of gases and dust that was farther across than the entire solar system is today. For a long time this dust cloud may have been formless, but at some point the force of gravity working within the cloud caused it to collapse into a flattened, revolving disk.

Today there are many theories that attempt to explain what happened within that huge dust cloud to form the sun and its planets. One theory suggests that the dust and gases near the center drew together to form the solar system's largest body, the sun. The planets formed in a similar way: most of the remainder broke up into gaseous proto-planets and the material in these contracted to form the planets.

Another theory holds that most of the material in the dust cloud went into the for-

The Fires Within Burst Out

Heat from inside the earth seeps out slowly through cracks in the surface, and now and then bursts out violently in the form of volcanoes and geysers. The steaming crater of Nyamlagira volcano in Africa (*left*) is a scene of broken rock and clouds of gas. The fiery fountains of Kilauea in Hawaii (*above*) spew forth a lava lake. It was lava from thousands of such eruptions underwater that built up volcanoes until they emerged as the Hawaiian Islands.

27

mation of what was to become the sun. As this "protosun" grew, it began spinning so fast that it cast off solid matter and gases that collected together to form the planets.

No matter which theory is eventually proved correct, the result is the same. At some point in the formation of the solar system, the sun began to shine; eventually the early solar wind blew free gases out of the solar system. After hundreds of millions of years had passed, what remained was the sun-warmed, shrunken inner planets and the gas-enveloped outer planets.

One bit of evidence that seems to support this theory is the orderliness of the solar system. For example, if the sun and all the planets were formed from the same spinning cloud of dust and gases, they would all tend to spin in the same direction. And they all do, except for Venus and Uranus, which for some unknown reason have reverse spins. However, all the planets travel in the same direction around the sun, and all are in a fairly flat plane around the sun's equator.

There is one exception: Pluto, the planet farthest from the sun, has an orbit that is extremely tilted to the central plane. Some scientists think it was once a moon of Neptune, its nearest neighbor, and escaped from its original orbit to become a planet in its own right. But until astronomers learn more about how the planets got their satellites, this is only an educated guess.

Until the earth could be weighed, no one could be sure what it was made of.

A Many-layered Sphere

If we could slice open the earth, we might see five distinct layers of matter beneath the crust, like those in the drawing at right. The crust is part of the lithosphere. Then come the asthenosphere and the mantle. All these layers are composed of denser and denser rock. Below these, most scientists believe, is an iron core divided into two parts. The outer core is liquid but the inner core is probably solid, due to the massive pressure on it. This core is the hottest part of the planet— the temperature there is believed to be between 4,000° F. and 8,000° F.

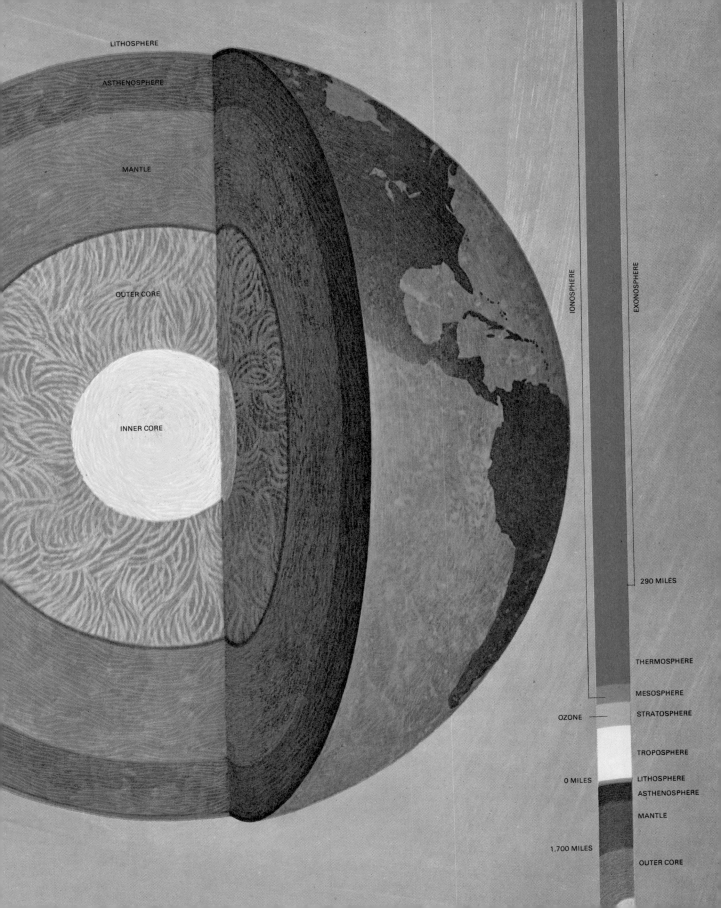

LITHOSPHERE

ASTHENOSPHERE

MANTLE

OUTER CORE

INNER CORE

IONOSPHERE

EXONOSPHERE

290 MILES

THERMOSPHERE

MESOSPHERE

OZONE ——— STRATOSPHERE

TROPOSPHERE

0 MILES LITHOSPHERE
ASTHENOSPHERE

MANTLE

1,700 MILES OUTER CORE

Steam from the Underworld

When the earth's underground water strikes hot rock, it turns into superheated steam, which forces its way through holes in the surface called fumaroles. This action is part of the earth's water cycle, in which water passes from the earth into the air, then falls again as rain, seeping under the ground or running in rivers to the sea.

But there were plenty of suggestions. One was that the earth was filled with water, and that it was this water, released by some terrible eruption, that caused the Biblical flood. Some people proposed that the earth's crust was dust, which floated on a bath of oil. Others believed the earth to be hollow, and perhaps filled with fire.

Finally, in 1798, the English physicist Henry Cavendish "weighed" the earth. Measuring the gravitational attraction between model spheres, and using a complex formula, he arrived at a weight of 6.6 sextillion (6.6 followed by 21 zeros) tons. As estimates go, it was a good one.

For its volume, which is about 260 billion cubic miles, the earth is the second densest planet in the solar system. Its average density is five and a half times that of water. (Saturn, at the other extreme, is so light it could float in water—if there were an ocean large enough to hold it.) But the average density of the rocks that make up the earth's outer layer, called the lithosphere, is too low to account for such a heavy planet. To the scientists who first thought about this, one fact immediately was clear: the density of the earth's interior had to be far greater than that of the surface rocks.

No one knows yet what lies beneath the earth's topmost shell. But scientists are learning, largely by studying earthquakes.

Although some earthquakes are powerful enough to break apart strong buildings, and others are nothing more than small tremors that pass unnoticed, the vibrations caused by quakes provide continuous information about the earth's interior. As a result of a century of study, seismologists (scientists who study earthquakes) know that nearly all major earthquakes occur along the edges of giant plates of lithosphere that move.

The principal zone is a belt in the lands that border the Pacific Ocean, running up the west coast of North and South America, and down the coast of Asia. The second major zone runs from west to east across Europe and Asia—from Spain, along northern Africa through Italy, Greece, Turkey, India and Burma—to join the Pacific belt. The first zone, known as the Pacific "ring of fire" because most of the world's volcanoes are along its path, is also the site of about 80 per cent of all earthquakes. The second zone is responsible for an additional 15 per cent or so. The remaining quakes occur at scattered locations elsewhere on the earth.

Nearly all earthquakes are caused by the fracturing, or breaking, of the rock of the earth's lithosphere along one or another of these zones. These fractures, called faults, occur when stresses that develop within the earth become too great for the rock to bear. A spectacular example is the San Andreas fault in California. The land mass west of the San Andreas fault is steadily inching its way north, but at some points, the rock becomes locked with rock on the other side of the fault. The stress at these points causes earthquakes. On April 18, 1906, the ground shift-

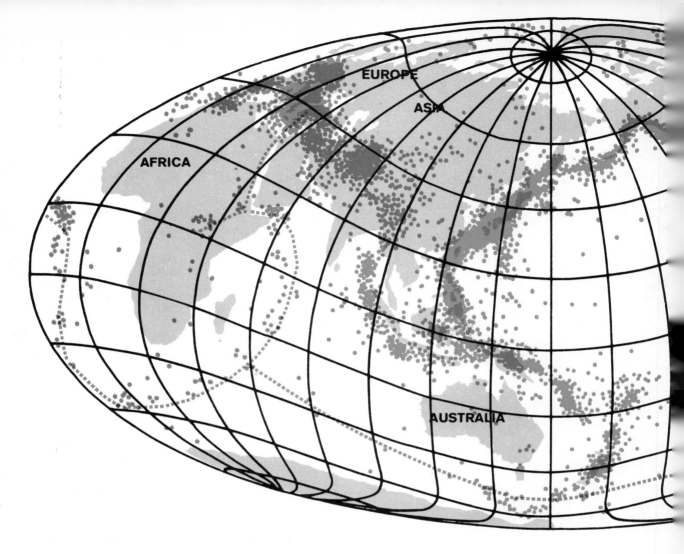

ed as much as 20 feet along 200-odd miles of the San Andreas fault, causing the earthquake that demolished much of San Francisco. It was one of the biggest earth shifts ever recorded for a single quake.

An earthquake is one of nature's most awesome events. The strongest earthquakes do not necessarily kill the most people, but when a major quake strikes in a heavily populated area, loss of life is enormous. The very violence of a quake may exceed the force of a billion tons of dynamite; while the most severe disturbance is local, the shock may be felt over wide areas. The major earthquake

that occurred in Guatemala in 1976, for example, not only killed almost 25,000 people and left a million homeless, but was felt as far north as Mexico City and damaged towns to the south in the neighboring countries of Honduras and El Salvador.

Similar devastation occurred in the historic Lisbon earthquake of 1755 that wrecked the heart of the city, killed thousands of its people, and made itself felt over a million and a half square miles of Europe. All over the Continent the waters of lakes and rivers were violently disturbed, and sea waves from the quake rushed all the way across

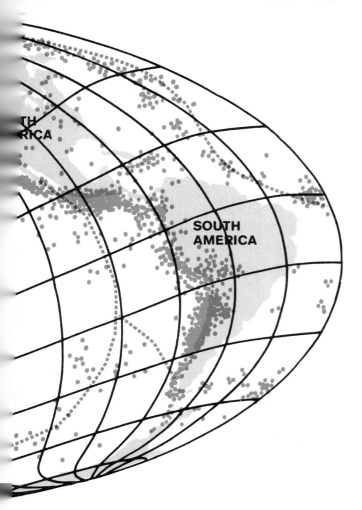

SOUTH
AMERICA

Where Earthquakes Occur

The clusters of dots on this map of the world show where major earthquakes have taken place over a period of 20 years. About 80 per cent of the quakes occur in a long belt around the rim of the Pacific Ocean. A second zone stretches from Spain across southern Europe and Asia to meet the Pacific group. A third belt runs under the oceans along a system of mountain ranges *(dotted line)* that indicate where land masses were once joined.

the Atlantic to the West Indies in a few hours. The quake occurred on November 1 —All Saints' Day—when the faithful all over Europe were in church. In the great cathedrals, awed spectators watched the chandeliers shake and swing to the shock waves from Lisbon.

The Lisbon quake was not the first by any means to have alarmed Europeans. But it was the most destructive by far, and the scale of the disaster reminded scientists how little they knew about the nature of earth tremors. One of them, the Emglish astronomer-mathematician John Michell, collected

all the reports he could find and was able to calculate that the shock wave had traveled at a speed of more than 20 miles a minute—1,200 miles per hour. Michell guessed that the source of the shock was an earth movement deep in the crust: ". . . it could not be much less than a mile or a mile and a half [deep]," he wrote, "and . . . it is probable that it did not exceed three miles."

Less than 30 years after the Lisbon disaster, a series of severe earthquakes convulsed the Calabrian district of southern Italy. The toll was far greater even than it had been in Lisbon—35,000 people lost their

33

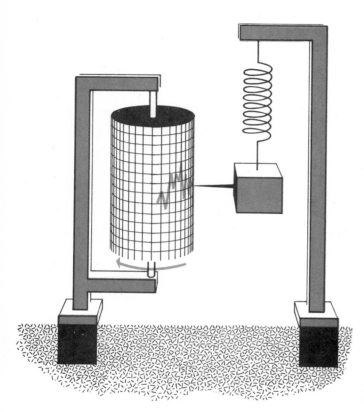

Tracing Quakes and Quivers

A seismograph, shown in simplified form in the drawing above, is an instrument that records the force and pattern of earthquakes. Its two metal frames are anchored solidly in rock. The frame at the left moves up and down with the earth's vibrations; at the same time its drum, fitted with graph paper, turns. Its movements are traced on the paper by the stylus, or pen, mounted on the heavy weight at right; this does not move because the coil spring above it absorbs the shocks.

lives. This second disaster served to bring more and more scientific effort to bear on the earthquake question. An urgent need was felt for some accurate scientific instrument that would measure the upheavals. It seemed possible that some new apparatus would not only supply missing information about the earthquakes themselves but also would provide vital information about the earth's unknown interior.

In 1855—a century after the Lisbon tragedy—the first seismograph was built, to record the force and pattern of earthquakes. Today thousands of these instruments are at work keeping track of rock movements all over the world. No single seismograph can show where an earthquake's tremors start. But each can tell the direction from which the tremors have come, and the distance away. Thus three seismographs at three different places can work together to pinpoint the exact location of the earthquake's center.

This new instrument soon showed that an earthquake's shock is transmitted in several different forms. The slowest is called a surface wave; it travels like an ocean wave along the curve of the earth's thin crust. Other waves drive straight into the body of the earth at a speed much greater than that of the surface waves. These deeper waves are of two kinds, primary—or P— and secondary—or S—waves. P waves are the faster and more penetrating, moving easily through the dense matter of the earth's interior. The slower-moving S waves disappear when they encounter liquids.

Therefore, when an earthquake has occurred the P waves—the fastest ones—are the first to show changes in the earth's vibration on a seismograph. Later the S waves arrive. Still later, the slower surface waves, journeying along the crust of the earth, make their squiggle on a seismograph's revolving drum. Seismographs can also point to the source and indicate the force of a volcanic eruption or of a nuclear explosion; and they play an extremely important role in predicting scientifically when an earthquake will occur in a certain area. Seismographs are in constant operation, and scientists have learned that P waves slow down for a time when an earthquake is brewing but resume their normal speed a short time before the quake happens.

Because these shock waves travel at different speeds as they move through different substances, scientists have been able to get a rough idea of what is inside the earth. They have learned, for example, that the earth's crust, which is the upper, or outer, part of the lithosphere, is an average of 20 miles thick beneath the continents. Under the oceans, however, the thickness of the crust is only about three miles.

The lithosphere as a whole is about 60 miles thick. Where the lithosphere ends and the upper mantle, called the asthenosphere, begins, the shock waves slow down. About 180 miles below the surface, the waves speed up again and, at a point 1,800 miles down, another abrupt change takes place. The fast-

E Marks the Earthquake

Seismographs in different cities are used together to pinpoint the exact center of an earthquake. Each instrument records the arrival of the vibrations that travel out from a quake. By measuring the time lapse between the primary and secondary shock waves, seismologists are able to estimate the distance traveled. Next, a circle with this distance as its radius is drawn around each city on a map. The single point at which all three circles cross is the earthquake's exact location or "epicenter" (E).

est P waves speed up even more, and the S waves simply disappear. This occurs at the region known as the outer core. Scientists believe it consists of iron (and some nickel) in liquid form—even though the inner core is thought to be hard. There are three basic reasons to think that this is so. For one thing, it is known that S waves can travel only through something rigid. Thus, the fact that they disappear when they travel deeper than 1,800 miles indicates that they have reached a liquid.

The second reason is that, to account for the total weight of the earth, both the outer and inner core must be composed of heavy metal. Further, the metal must be enormously compressed. In fact it is estimated that the iron and nickel in the earth's core weigh 750 pounds per cubic foot. The same volume of these metals on the earth's surface weighs 250 pounds less.

The core must also be very hot. Most scientists today think that its temperature is somewhere between 4,000 and 8,000 degrees Fahrenheit. But since there is a layer of insulating rock, nearly 2,000 miles thick, between the core and the surface, the heat is contained deep within the earth.

The third, and perhaps the most important reason, is based on evidence that has been found in meteorites—meteors that have landed on earth. Most meteorites contain a great deal of metallic iron; some, in fact, are almost totally composed of iron. Meteors are a part of the solar system, and were probably formed in the same way as the planets (although on a much smaller scale), and of the same materials. Therefore, scientists reason, if meteorites contain large amounts of metallic iron, so must the earth.

Human beings will probably never be able to visit these strange regions deep inside our planet. But the more scientists discover about the interior the more they will be able to learn about the origins of the earth, and even of the entire solar system.

There is another reason why scientists are eager to know what is in the interior of this planet. They hope to find out how the earth's magnetic field works.

The magnetic compass has been used by sailors for nearly a thousand years. At first many people thought that its needle was attracted by the constellation known as the Great Bear, or perhaps by Polaris, the North Star. Some even thought that a huge mountain caused the needle to point north. But in the year 1600 an Englishman named William Gilbert showed that the earth itself acted as a huge magnet.

Scientists now believe that the earth's magnetism is generated by the mass of molten iron that they think forms the core of the planet. This theory provides yet another reason to think that the core is indeed a hot mass of metal.

The earth's magnetic field is strange and unpredictable, however. For one thing, the north magnetic pole moves. Not only is it several hundred miles from the true North Pole, but in the past half century it has

Damage from Shifting Rock

Earthquakes occur when movement in the lithosphere causes the brittle surface rock to break. One section of the lithosphere shifts in relation to another—which is what happened under a once-straight railroad track in California *(left)*. Such events produce powerful shock waves. These shake the earth and may cause buildings to lurch or topple and fires to break out, as they did during a severe earthquake in 1948 in Fukui, Japan *(below)*.

moved some 250 miles to the northwest. And the magnetic field does not have a constant strength. In fact, it has been growing weaker—in the last 100 years its power has decreased by 5 per cent.

There is recent evidence that the earth's magnetic field undergoes even more startling changes. The field periodically reverses itself—the north and south magnetic poles exchange places. These reversals have occurred irregularly at least five times in the last four million years.

The evidence to support this theory has been found in iron-bearing rocks in the earth's crust. Because the atoms in iron molecules act as tiny magnets, the grains of iron in these rocks become aligned in the direction of the field when the rocks are being formed. When the magnetic poles shift, the atoms remain pointing, like arrows, toward the earlier pole. By determining the age of these rocks, geologists can determine when the poles exchanged places.

What happens when the magnetic poles reverse? Compasses, of course, will continue to point to the north magnetic pole, wherever it is—even if it is located in Antarctica, at the geographic South Pole. But the earth's magnetic field does not only serve as a handy guide for mariners and explorers. It is also responsible for shielding the earth from bombardment by cosmic rays and particles emitted by the sun and other stars. If the magnetic field weakens, more of this radiation can get through to

Slicing Life of Long Ago

Land under the ocean floor contains fossils that help us understand the history of life on earth. The long cylinder in the picture above is a core of clay brought up from hundreds of feet under the water. A paleontologist is slicing the core into sections, so that the fossils can be removed and studied.

Measuring Earthly Tides

The earth's crust, in addition to cracking in earthquakes, is constantly stretching and tightening up, because the moon's attraction creates "tides" on solid land as well as on oceans. The instrument shown here, called a strain meter, measures these movements deep inside a mountain.

reach the earth's surface. And scientists believe that in the process of reversing itself the field is weakened; just how long the weakening lasts is not yet known.

Even with a strong magnetic field, not all radiation is blocked from reaching the earth. The plants and animals—including human beings—that now live on the earth have adapted to this radiation. But what would happen to living things if the radiation were to increase? An overdose of charged particles, for example, can damage living cells. If reproductive cells are damaged, the genetic structure of those cells—which determines heredity—may be altered, in a process known as mutation.

Scientists have searched for evidence of such an evolutionary change, evidence that would indicate that great numbers of mutations occurred at the times the magnetic field changed. Indications are that if such an increase in radiation does occur it is probably slight. One investigator has likened the difference to that found by a person who moves from Los Angeles to Denver—that is, from a city at sea level to one that is a mile above sea level. People who live in Denver are shielded by a blanket of atmosphere one mile less deep than are those who live in Los Angeles—yet no one has found that mutations occur more often in Denver.

But scientists have made an interesting discovery involving plankton, a tiny, simple form of animal life that lives in the oceans. By digging into the sea floor and obtaining fossils of plankton, they have found that when the magnetic field reversed itself, older types of plankton seemed to die out, to be replaced by newer types. There is no clear-cut explanation for this phenomenon, but the fact that it did occur indicates that there may be some connection between the changing forms of plankton and the shift in the magnetic field.

What force causes these mysterious shifts in the earth's magnetic field? Only recently it was discovered that 700,000 years ago—exactly when the last reversal took place—a gigantic meteor struck the earth, landing in the continent of Antarctica. This occurrence may merely be a coincidence: scientists do not yet know the answer.

A Crack that Means Danger

The dark line in this aerial photograph is a part of the 600-mile-long San Andreas fault, a large crack in the earth in California. The land to the west (*right*) is inching northward. The strain created makes the surface crack from time to time, causing earthquakes like the one in San Francisco in 1906.

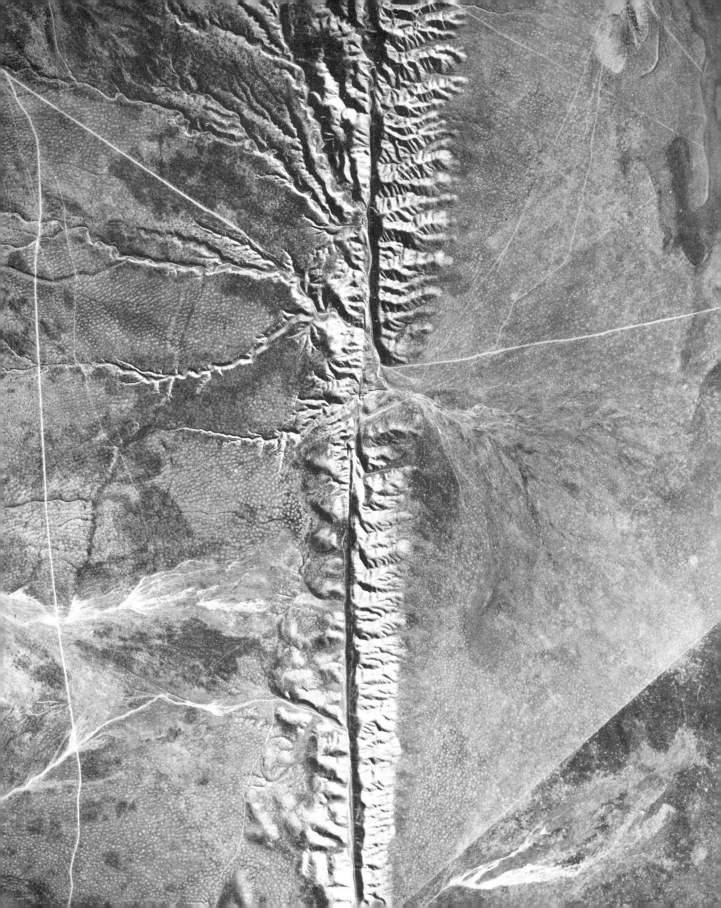

TOWERING THUNDERCLOUDS pour rain into the
Pacific Ocean off the island of Samoa. The lowest
clouds, from which the rain seems to be falling, are
only the very bottom of the heap; thunderstorms
like this one often extend from just above the
ocean to an altitude of more than eight miles.

3

The Mighty Engine
of the Atmosphere

The sea, which covers nearly three quarters of the globe, is only the second biggest thing on earth. Much larger is the ocean of the atmosphere, which dominates the lives of men and all other creatures as surely as water dominates the lives of fish. Without the atmosphere's oxygen living things die almost at once. Without rain erosion and the weathering of rocks there

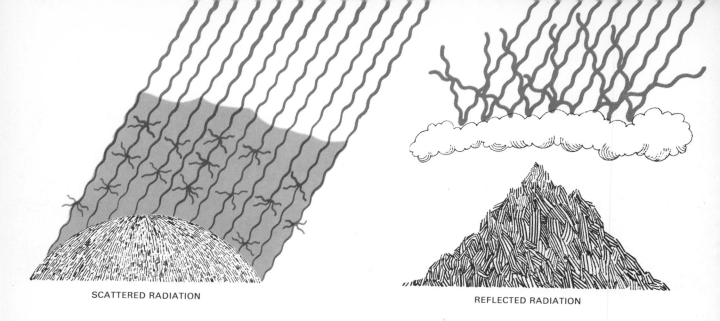

SCATTERED RADIATION

REFLECTED RADIATION

would be no soil for plants to grow in. Without carbon dioxide the plants could not produce carbohydrates, the primary link in the food chain that supports all animal life. Without the high-altitude umbrella of ozone to absorb the deadly ultraviolet rays of the sun, human existence—if any—would be quite different. Yet this is only a small list of the free services performed by the atmosphere and taken for granted by more than three billion human beings who at this moment are drawing breaths of it.

The atmosphere is an invisible mixture of gases—nitrogen, oxygen, carbon dioxide and water vapor make up most of the ocean of air. It also contains dust particles and the waste products of men, such as soot and radioactive fallout particles from nuclear explosions. At sea level a cubic foot of this mixture weighs about an ounce and a quarter, but because of the force with which gravity holds it in place, the atmosphere exerts a pressure of about 15 pounds per square inch at sea level. The

human body and, of course, animals and plants balance this pressure by exerting an equal outward pressure. Just as water pressure is greatest at the bottom of the sea, so atmospheric pressure is greatest at the bottom of the ocean of air. The greater the altitude the less the pressure, and the thinner the atmosphere becomes. The ocean of air is dense enough at a height of 12 miles to support airplanes and balloons. It continues to thin out at higher altitudes until at a point many hundreds of miles above the earth's surface it blends with the almost total emptiness of space.

Meteorologists, the scientists who study the atmosphere and its weather patterns, have found that the atmosphere is divided into four basic parts according to temperatures. They are known as the troposphere, the stratosphere, the mesosphere and the thermosphere. The troposphere is the bottom layer, and it supports all life. Its upper boundary is as low as five miles above the Poles, about 10 miles above the equator. Everywhere within the troposphere the air is a

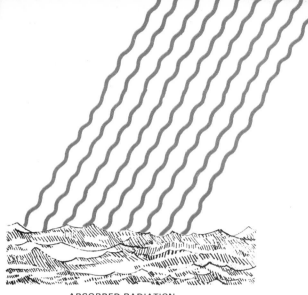

ABSORBED RADIATION

Sunpower to Run the Earth

Of the sun's total radiation, only a small fraction is aimed at the earth. But that amount is more than enough to keep our planet running. Some of the radiation is scattered by air, dust and water vapor in the atmosphere (*far left*). Clouds reflect about 25 per cent of the radiation (*center*). The remainder (*left*) heats the earth's surface, which in turn re-radiates the energy to heat the atmosphere and thus run the world's vast weather machine.

constant mixture: nitrogen 78 per cent, oxygen 21 per cent, argon 0.9 per cent, carbon dioxide 0.03 per cent—with traces of half a dozen other gases plus some water vapor.

Starting in the stratosphere, a layer reaching 20 miles higher, and in the mesosphere, which goes up to an altitude of 50 miles or so, there are important chemical changes in the air. In both layers, ozone is added to the mix. An uncommon form of oxygen, ozone is generated when an electrical discharge or strong ultraviolet rays pass through ordinary oxygen. In the upper atmosphere, ozone soaks up much of the ultraviolet radiation streaming earthward from the sun.

Starting at 50 miles above the earth and reaching to the edge of space is the ionosphere, in which high-energy rays from the sun ionize the air, electrically charging atoms and molecules, and freeing electrons. The air here is terribly thin, but it is this layer that reflects radio waves back to earth, making possible long-distance broadcasts.

The outermost layer of all, which begins at about 300 miles above the earth, is called the exosphere. Although it is a part of our atmosphere—it falls within the thermosphere—it is not composed of air as we know it.

The inner portion of the exosphere is a 900-mile-thick layer of helium, the same gas that is used to inflate the toy balloons youngsters clamor for in parks and at circuses. Beyond the helium is the outer part of the exosphere, a layer of hydrogen. Both the helium and hydrogen layers are extremely rarefied—so much so that individual molecules, which collide frequently at sea level, seldom even touch one another. And in the outer regions of the thin exosphere, some 2,000 miles from the surface of the earth, particles from the earth's atmosphere are able to escape into interplanetary space.

From this quick tour, working from the inside out, it is apparent that the atmosphere is a very important part of the earth. Its major action is to serve as an enormous engine, using the sun's radiation as a power source to drive the currents of air that stream and eddy around the earth.

Although it is the sun's power that runs the atmospheric engine, the power is not applied directly. The sun does not heat the air. In fact, much of the radiation from the sun—the radiation we see as light and feel as heat—passes right through the air, striking and warming the planet's surface. It is the earth itself that heats the air from below, in much the same way that a pot of water is heated over the flames of the stove.

The earth's surface is not warmed the same amount everywhere by the sun's rays. Sunlight strikes the earth more directly at the equator than it does at the Poles, so the air near the equator is warmer than the air to the north or south. It is this difference in the temperature of the air that turns the atmosphere into an engine: the warm air, being lighter, rises, while the heavier cold air moves in to take its place, causing the winds to blow.

If the earth did not rotate, these air cur-

A Cold Front Barges In

Forcing its way beneath a mass of warm light air, a cool, heavier air mass travels from left to right in the illustration below. Because it is lighter, the warmer air is pushed upward by the cooler air. As it rises, the warm air cools and the water vapor it contains condenses to form thunderclouds and rain, which occur along the cold front.

WARM AIR MASS

COLD AIR MASS

rents would be quite orderly: warm air near the equator would rise and flow toward the Poles, while cold air at the Poles would sink and flow toward the equator in an endless cycle. The earth's rotation modifies this simple pattern: in each hemisphere, working away from the Pole and toward the equator, there is first a westward drift of air in the lower atmosphere, then an eastward one in mid-latitudes, and finally another westward drift near the equator. The pattern of air flow in each hemisphere is a mirror image of the pattern in the other: the easterly winds of the northern tropics—the "trade winds"—blow from the northeast, while the same easterly trades below the equator blow from the southeast. The name trade wind originated in the days of sailing ships, when these steady winds were the mainstay of ocean commerce.

The westerly winds of middle latitudes (the United States falls into this region) do not share the trade winds' regular, stable pattern. Instead, they are rolled into im-

A Warm Front Creeps Up

Like a cold front, a warm front often brings rain. But while the arrival of a cold front with its wall of thunderclouds is dramatic, the arrival of a warm front is quiet and relatively gentle. The lighter, warmer air slides up over the cool air mass, causing rain, and forming wispy, high altitude clouds that may appear several days before the front arrives.

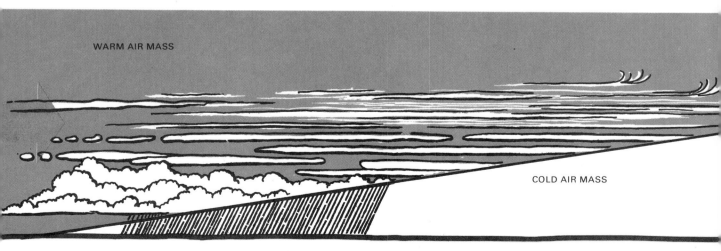

WARM AIR MASS

COLD AIR MASS

New York Masked in Haze . . .

Warm, moist tropical air, which has moved in from
the Atlantic Ocean to the south, combines with
New York's smoke to form a thick blanket of
"smaze," as a mixture of smoke and haze is
sometimes called. This photograph was taken from
a skyscraper on 50th Street. The Empire State
Building, only 16 blocks away, can barely be seen.

mense high-altitude eddies, thousands of
miles across. Below these large-scale eddies
(three to six of which are over each hemisphere at any one time) are many smaller
ones that swirl about for a few hours or
days before they vanish and are replaced
by others. The larger eddies are more per-
sistent: one of them may move eastward
for weeks before breaking up. The birth
and growth of these wind swirls account
for the changeable weather of the earth's
middle latitudes.

A smaller eddy that forms around a center of low-pressure air acquires a rotary
motion and starts to spin—counterclockwise
in the Northern Hemisphere and clockwise
south of the equator. Such a spinning eddy
is called a cyclone, but is not necessarily
the storm wind that is sometimes known

by the same name. Here is a chance to watch the atmosphere's heat engine in action on a small scale. Why does a cyclone spin? The air at its center is lighter and lower in pressure while the air surrounding the eddy is heavier and higher in pressure. Thus, the heavier air flows *inward*, toward the center, and it is this inward flow that is deflected by the rotation of the earth. Consider the opposite case: the eddy forms around a deep, dense air mass at higher pressure than the air around it, and the air flow is therefore *outward* from its center. In consequence, the spin is in exactly the opposite direction and such an eddy is known as an anticyclone.

These great whorls of air make the major marks on weather maps. The United States is often swept in winter by high pressure

. . . Reappears When It Clears

A mass of cool, dry polar air has moved in from the north, pushing the unpleasant smaze before it, and the view is now measured in miles rather than in blocks. But the cooler air does not always arrive immediately; New York and other industrialized, smoke-producing cities are often bathed for days at a time in the fumes of their own air pollution.

CIRRUS: 20,000 TO 40,000 FEET

CUMULUS: 8,000 FEET TO 45,000 FEET FROM BASE TO TOP

ALTOCUMULUS: 8,000 TO 20,000 FEET

CIRROCUMULUS: 20,000 TO 40,000 FEET

The Language of Clouds

For thousands of years men have "read" clouds for signs of changing weather. The three basic types of cloud are *cirrus* (Latin for "curl of hair"), *cumulus* ("pile") and *stratus* ("spread out"). Among the highest clouds (*top row*) are *cirrus*, whose wisps of tiny ice crystals indicate a far-off storm. *Cirrocumulus*, sometimes called a "mackerel sky," herald a cold front; *cirrostratus*, seen as a halo around the sun, mean that rain is likely. At middle altitudes float the puffy *cumulus*, which may grow into *cumulonimbus*, or "thunderheads." Still lower, *altocumulus* may be a sign of rain and *altostratus* often indicate prolonged rain or snow. The lowest clouds (*bottom row*) include the thick, dark *nimbostratus*, which bring continuous rain or snow; the flat, gray *stratus*, which are accompanied by a drizzle or snow flurries; and the wavy *stratocumulus*, which may drop a light sprinkling of snow.

NIMBOSTRATUS: BELOW 8,000 FEET

STRATUS: BELOW 8,000 FEET

CIRROSTRATUS: 20,000 TO 40,000 FEET

⌐UMULONIMBUS: 10,000 TO 60,000 FEET FROM BASE TO TOP

ALTOSTRATUS: 8,000 TO 20,000 FEET

STRATOCUMULUS: BELOW 8,000 FEET

systems from northern Canada that are very cold and dry. When such a cold air mass overlies a region, the weather will be cold and clear. In summer, moist lows from the Gulf of Mexico often dominate weather in the eastern United States, producing hot, humid, windless days.

The line of contact between two air masses of different temperature is called a "front." A cold front represents cold air replacing warmer air; a warm front moves in such a way that warm air replaces cold. The warm air along a front of either kind cools as it rises, producing cloudiness and precipitation. This effect is more noticeable along a cold front, which usually leads to more violent storms. The approach and passage of a front is signaled by cirrus clouds— "mare's-tails"—high in the sky. Soon a milky film of cirrostratus covers the sky, and some hours later the ominous gray veils of altostratus clouds appear. Then low, thick, dark nimbostratus clouds darken the sky and rain begins to fall. Finally the warm air completely replaces the cold, from top to bottom, the temperature levels off and the rain stops. More or less steady weather then follows until the approach of the next front.

The sequence of events when a cold front arrives is faster and often more dramatic. The cold oncoming air is too heavy to override the warm air in its path, and burrows underneath instead. Forced upward by the cold air mass, the warm moisture-laden air

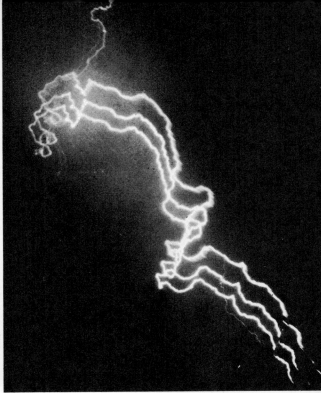

condenses, forming a great vertical bank of dense cumulonimbus clouds. A well-defined cold front usually appears as a squall line of dark clouds, straight as a ruler from horizon to horizon, sweeping in from the west or northwest. When it strikes, the wind shifts abruptly from southwest to northwest, the temperature falls and a torrent of heavy rain begins, driven by strong, irregular gusts. A violent thunderstorm may occur, adding sight and sound to the tempestuous proceedings. After half an hour or so the squall line is almost out of sight to the east, and a band of clear sky appears in the west. Then the northwest wind blows more steadily, and dry, cool, clear weather sets in. Of course, not all cold fronts bring with them such boisterous effects, but the pattern is familiar to dwellers in the middle latitudes.

The turbulent, unstable atmosphere near a squall line sometimes produces a vortex of rapidly spinning air. The vortex appears as a narrow, funnel-shaped cloud that extends to the ground and that conceals winds of hundreds of miles an hour. A vortex of this kind is called a tornado on land and a waterspout over the ocean. Very little is known about conditions inside the whirlwinds, because any instruments that have happened to be in their paths have always been destroyed.

Few people have looked such a whirlwind in the "eye" and lived to tell about it. One who did was Will Keller, a Kansas farmer who dared to peek out of his storm cellar as a tornado passed over in 1928. Above him was the hollow vortex, 50 to 100 feet across, its walls lighted by zigzag lightning flashes. Smaller vortexes were forming inside the main one and emitting

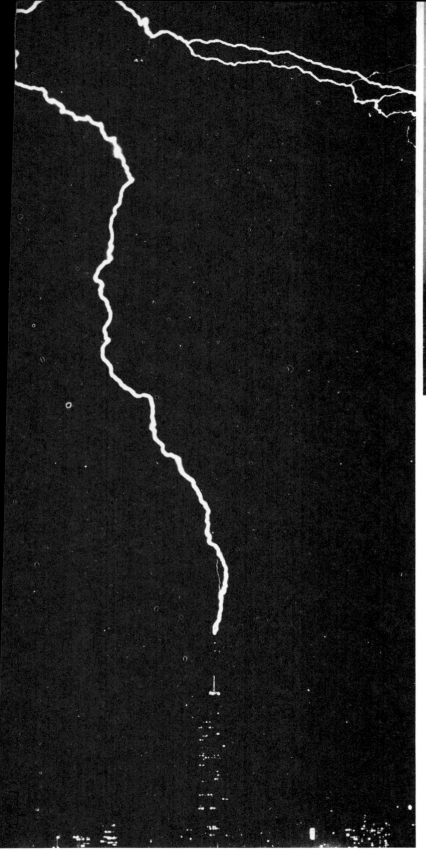

When Lightning Strikes

Lightning occurs when there is enough difference in the electrical charge of clouds and earth for a "spark" to jump the gap. At far left, the sky, as seen from a forest ranger's tower, is filled with a series of lightning flashes. Next to this is a picture showing a triple stroke made by flashes only fractions of a second apart. Lightning is usually attracted to the tallest object in the area. One of the hundreds of lightning bolts that strike the Empire State Building harmlessly each year is shown at left; above, a bolt is even attracted to a tower of water thrown up by the explosion of a Navy depth charge.

hissing noises as they broke free of it.

Usually a tornado is a few hundred yards across and travels at perhaps 25 miles per hour for a distance anywhere from a fraction of a mile to 100 miles or more before it vanishes. The central United States probably has more tornadoes than any other part of the world, and they form so rapidly and unpredictably that about the only protection against them is to climb into a strong storm cellar whenever a thunderstorm appears. Waterspouts are generally milder than tornadoes, though still capable of violent destruction. The lower portion of a spout contains some salt water drawn up from the sea beneath it, but consists mostly of fresh water that has condensed out from its basic body of cloud. Some waterspouts range up to a mile in height.

Many localities have other peculiar winds of their own that are more or less unrelated to the global pattern. Simple examples are the sea and land breezes familiar along many coast lines. These winds owe their existence to the fact that the temperature of the ocean surface stays fairly constant while that of the land surface may fluctuate widely. On a hot day a beach becomes warm and the air above it rises while cooler, denser air from over the water—the sea breeze —is drawn in to replace it. At night the beach cools rapidly and the air circulation is reversed: the air over the land is now denser, and a land breeze flows offshore.

The sea and land breezes' grown-up relatives are the monsoons of Asia, which are

A Twister's Fearful Path

A tornado thunders down a Texas highway. Wherever its whirling tip touches down, it leaves destruction; bits of houses, which have been pulled apart and flung into the air, are visible in the photograph above. The damage a twister does is often freakish. It may level an entire city block, yet leave one house standing. Or, as in the case of the Iowa farmyard at right, it can destroy a barn, tear the top from a silo—and leave five horses unhurt, still standing in the wreckage of their stalls.

governed by the contrasts in land and sea temperatures in summer and winter, instead of in daytime and nighttime. In winter the Asiatic plateau is bitterly cold, so that the overlying air is much denser than that above the China Sea and the Indian Ocean to its east and south. A steady cold, dry wind blows offshore from October to April, deflected by the earth's rotation into a northeast wind in the China Sea and in the northern part of the Indian Ocean. In the summer, Asia swelters and the air above it rises, while cooler air moves in from the ocean. This summer "monsoon" brings air that has picked up a considerable amount of moisture as it crossed the sea, and its arrival deluges southeast Asia with prolonged, drenching rain. A monsoon climate of this kind has only two varieties of weather, wet in summer and dry in winter, in contrast to the changing weather of middle-latitude weather.

Other regional winds are conditioned by landscape as well as temperature. Cold, dry air may spill over a mountain range suddenly after having collected on the windward side of the range for some time, surging down into adjacent valleys with great force. The "mistral," a French wind, consists of cold air from the Rhone Glacier that pours down the Rhone river valley to the sea for much of the year, while the "bora" of the Adriatic rushes out of the mountains of Yugoslavia. The geography of the Mediterranean—the sea is bordered by high mountains on the north and the hot Sahara on the south—is responsible for a number of notorious winds. At times a hot wind from the Sahara, the "sirocco," blows north across the Mediterranean, accumulating enough water vapor along the way to bring rain to Sicily and the Italian coast.

Those who live along the fringes of the world's oceans have good reason to fear the coming of fall, when tropical cyclones are most likely to be born at sea and to cause disaster if they sweep over the land. The western shores of the North Atlantic, the North and South Pacific, and the Indian Oceans are most often the targets of tropical cyclones. They are unknown only in the South Atlantic and in the eastern part of the South Pacific. These violent tropical storms are quite rare (only an average of about 50 of them occur each year in the entire world), but their high power sets them apart, along with earthquakes, as the most destructive of natural phenomena.

At birth, one of these typhoons or hurricanes forms as a zone of low atmospheric pressure over a tropical ocean. Warm air laden with moisture flows toward this zone and rises within it. The water vapor in the rising column of warm air condenses into clouds and rain, freeing a great deal of heat in the process, which further speeds the upward flow of air. Perhaps a quarter of a million tons of water are extracted from the ocean and the air every *second* by a hurricane, and their condensation over

Tracking a Hurricane

From high above the earth the travels of a hurricane are closely watched. A weather satellite streaking over the southern United States took the photograph at right, which was relayed to the ground by radio. The outline of the Florida coastline placed over the picture shows the center of the storm to be north of Jacksonville. A radar installation at Miami also tracked the hurricane (*above*). Miami is at the center of the radar screen, and the calm, cloudless "eye" of the storm is about 75 miles to the north of the city.

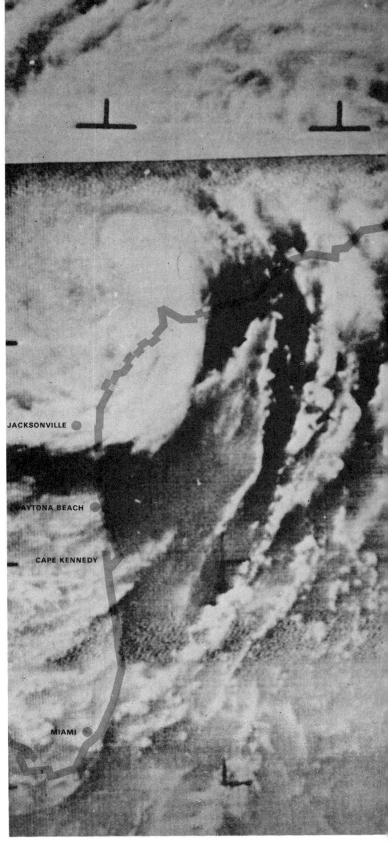

one day releases energy equivalent to the explosion of a 13,000-megaton nuclear bomb. As the heated air rises faster and faster, new air converges on the storm center with ever increasing speed; winds of as much as 200 miles per hour may be generated in this way.

The hurricane itself is a nightmare of shrieking wind accompanied by torrents of rain and darkness, as dense clouds blot out the sky. If the "eye" passes overhead, the turmoil becomes increasingly louder, then abruptly stops; the wind falls to a breeze, the rain ceases and bits of blue sky appear through thin, patchy clouds. But the lull is brief and soon the full fury of the storm

strikes again, now with the wind from the opposite direction.

Such a storm is fueled by the heat and water vapor that it sucks up from the sea surface, and it weakens and disappears in short order when it is deprived of this power supply. Thus hurricanes seldom penetrate far inland, and if they miss land

A Storm Hits Cape Cod

Huge seas, raised by an ocean storm, batter the waterfront of Provincetown, Massachusetts, at the tip of Cape Cod. Every year the cape is beset by such storms, which slowly wear away the sand dunes facing the Atlantic. The same storms add sand to the side that faces sheltered Cape Cod Bay.

entirely by swinging toward the Pole, the colder water in their paths quenches their violence before long.

In a single year the engine of the atmosphere, using such forceful instruments as typhoons and monsoons and such peaceful ones as sunlight, lifts 100,000 cubic miles of water into the air from the sea and the continents. Everything that goes up in this massive evaporation process must eventually come down, and most of it precipitates as rain.

In order for rain, snow, sleet or hail to fall, clouds must form. Even air that is supersaturated with moisture cannot usually produce clouds unless countless numbers of tiny "condensation nuclei" are present. The nuclei may be particles of salt from sea spray, or fine dust, or smoke particles from forest fires and industrial plants, or the combustion products of volcanoes. It has been estimated that the eruption in 1883 on the volcanic island of Krakatoa, in the North Pacific Ocean, filled the atmosphere with enough condensation nuclei to provide 1,000 rainy days throughout the world.

The water-vapor molecules that join a nucleus form cloud droplets (or ice crystals, if the air is well below freezing). These cannot fall as rain: they hold only a millionth as much water as an ordinary raindrop. In absolutely still air they would take eight hours to fall a quarter of a mile, and in moving air they are hardly affected by gravity at all. It is their growth to bigger size that makes precipitation possible. In turbulent air bigger droplets collide with and "collect" smaller ones; in cold air, droplets evaporate and then condense on nearby ice crystals.

Only when a droplet grows to raindrop size, at least 1/125th of an inch in diameter, can it fall out of the cloud. It may never reach the ground; often a torrent may spill out of clouds high above a desert, only to evaporate entirely on the way down. Raindrops that reach the earth in a fine spray, called drizzle, have fallen from relatively low clouds, with little time to collide with other drops while falling. The raindrops that arrive in a vigorous downpour come from deep clouds where the colliding of droplets, and the "capturing" of little ones by bigger ones, is going on quite actively.

A Fountain of Color

The thunderstorm is almost over in the Arizona desert. Suddenly the lingering gray clouds part, and the afternoon sunlight streams forth. As the bright rays shine through the last of the rain, each drop acts as a prism, splitting the white light into every color of the spectrum, signaling the storm's end.

4

Erosion: Forces That Shape the Land

It is not every day that a newborn volcano shoots lava out of a cornfield or an island sinks beneath the waves or an earthquake crumbles a city. While the earth is forever rearranging its features, most of its changes of face are leisurely rather than catastrophic. A human lifetime simply does not offer a long enough look to make most of the changes apparent. So until a few generations ago most people assumed that the landscape was here to stay. The hills were thought to be eternal, or as William Cullen Bryant put it, "ancient as the sun."

But 19th Century geologists already were taking closer looks at the earth around them and beginning to find clues that had been available all along. Shore lines everywhere were advancing or retreating; the brink of Niagara Falls was receding a few feet every year; some "eternal" hills were

THE BADLANDS of South Dakota are a spectacular result of erosion, Nature's tool for flattening and carving the face of the earth. The jagged, crumpled landscape of clay and sandstone was once smooth and sloping, part of the Great Plains of the Midwest that begin at the eastern edge of the Rocky Mountains.

63

1. RAINWATER   2. ACIDS FROM LICHENS   3. FROST AND RAIN

decaying while others appeared to be on the rise. In time it was realized that even the splash of a single raindrop on the soil counted for something in the remolding of the earth.

During this reappraisal of the landscape the ruins of the Greek temple of Serapis at Pozzuoli, near Naples, were excavated. When this building was studied by scientists, it was found that several of its columns were still standing upright and that three of them were riddled with holes drilled by a species of borer clam that is still common in the nearby Mediterranean. What was puzzling was that some of these holes were bored near the tops of the columns, and there was no known way that clams could have climbed up there. The mystery was not settled until men finally

believed what the evidence clearly showed: the temple had been engulfed by the sea when the land under it sank. The borer clams did their work, and later on the temple rose again, its columns still upright.

Nothing else on the face of the globe, it turns out, is unchangeable either. For two major sets of forces are engaged in a titanic contest, of which the pioneer Scottish geologist James Hutton said: "We find no sign of a beginning—no prospect of an end." These are the tearing-down forces of weathering and erosion and the uplifting forces that begin deep within the earth.

Weathering and erosion include all of the processes by which rock is worn away and its debris deposited somewhere else. The uplifting forces are called diastrophism, from the Greek meaning "thorough turning over." It refers to the processes by which

64

4. CRACK ETCHING

5. FROST

6. WIND AND WATER

the earth's crust is uplifted, tilted, fractured and folded and dragged down from below. If either erosion or diastrophism ever gained full power, this would become an unrecognizable world. Erosion would wash most of North America into the oceans within 25 million years, leaving only a wide, low plain, which ultimately might be entirely covered by the sea. Diastrophism would contort the earth's surface into contours as jagged as the mountains of the moon. Such things do not happen, because a balance of power exists between erosion and diastrophism, although it is far from peaceful.

Once the nature of the struggle between the two forces of erosion and diastrophism was understood, scientists were able to clear up most of the mystery of the earth's topography. The jumbled rocks were given meaning and could be understood.

Weathering and Erosion

Weather changes the earth's landscape by tearing down rock in various ways, some of which are shown here. (1) Rainwater made vertical cracks in muddy, sandy rock to carve the spectacular pillars of Bryce Canyon. (2) Acids, manufactured by red lichen plants, have eaten into a volcanic rock. (3) Frost and rainwater modeled this strange stone sculpture in Utah. (4) Heat and moisture have rounded the original cracks of a large block of granite, creating a smooth rock stack. (5) Water in the cracks of the rock has frozen and expanded, loosening chunks from a cliff face. (6) Wind in the Sahara in Africa has swept away particles of soft rock loosened by water, producing weird forms.

The sources of the great heavings that lift up the mountains are deeply hidden from view. But most of the agents of erosion work openly for all to see. The greatest of these is running water. The atmosphere sucks up about 100,000 cubic miles of moisture every year. Most of this falls back into the oceans, but about 35,000 cubic miles of it reaches the land as rain, snow, sleet, hail and dew. A great deal of this water goes underground, and a great deal more evaporates again before flowing very far, but an estimated 10 million billion gallons run off to resupply the seas. This is the flood that year after year does the most to reshape the land.

It is not so much the water itself that does the work, but the particles and chemicals that it carries along. The change in color from a clear, swift mountain stream to the slow, brown currents of a major river shows how each tributary adds its portion of particles to the main stream's load. The Mississippi River system, for example, drains an area of about a million and a quarter square miles. In a year, something over 600 million tons of mud, clay, mineral fragments and pinpoint-sized lumps of rock are carried down and dropped into the Gulf of Mexico. From the first flake of mica swirling in a mountain brook to the last quartz sand grain stripped from a downstream bar, each particle serves as one of the Mississippi system's erosive teeth, nibbling at riverbanks and bottoms along the way.

The speed of water's flow is a vital factor in the erosive power of streams. A youthful, steep mountain torrent, flowing about 10 feet a second, not only carries fine particles in suspension and mineral salts in solution, but also rolls, pushes and tumbles masses of pebbles, gravel and even boulders downhill along its bed. As the grade levels off and the water loses velocity, the larger stones are left behind, then the smaller ones. A stream is a kind of sorting machine, grading its suspended load with fair precision. Coarse materials fall out first, gravels and sands reaching the bottom and the banks long before the finer fragments of mud can sink.

Most often a great river valley begins as tiny channels in the soft surfaces of hillsides. With each rainfall the channels are deepened by runoff water until they become gullies. The stream always follows the shortest and easiest path downhill. As it grows bigger, the stream can carry more and more grinding materials and its cutting force increases.

In time the rapids and waterfalls of the young river eat away the irregularities in its bed, and the resulting gentler slope reduces the current's vigor. As they age, streams that were once swift and straight broaden out their narrow, steep-sided valleys. They turn into old rivers like the Yellow and the Mississippi, meandering sluggishly across broad valleys. These valleys are smooth and flat because of the burden of mud and silt distributed by the

A Plateau's Eventful Past

A "stairway" of eroded land in the Colorado Plateau shows different ages of rock, from the youngest layer at Bryce Canyon to the oldest at the bottom of the Grand Canyon. After the Precambrian period *(bottom layer)*, warm, shallow seas repeatedly covered the area, disappearing and returning. These seas deposited layers of hard-packed sand and mud on the lowest bedrock. About 10 million years ago, a mighty force raised the entire area thousands of feet above sea level. Since then, rains and rivers have gradually exposed the rock as they chiseled the landscape into the formations that we see today.

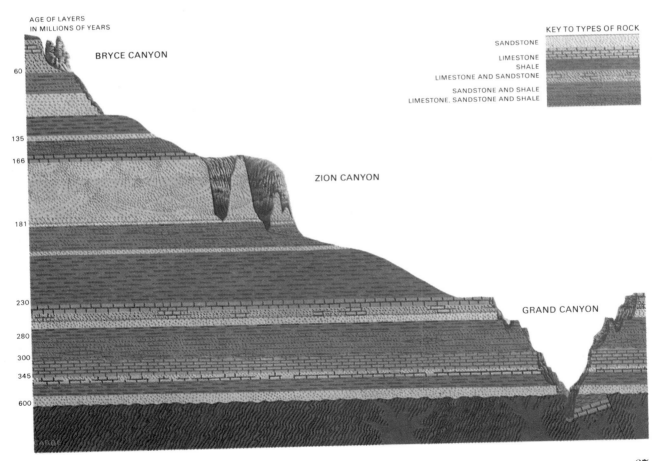

AGE OF LAYERS
IN MILLIONS OF YEARS

BRYCE CANYON

ZION CANYON

GRAND CANYON

60

135

166

181

230

280

300

345

600

KEY TO TYPES OF ROCK

SANDSTONE
LIMESTONE
SHALE
LIMESTONE AND SANDSTONE
SANDSTONE AND SHALE
LIMESTONE, SANDSTONE AND SHALE

67

Carving a Limestone Cave

Eerie caves like the Carlsbad Caverns in New Mexico (*left*) are formed by the erosion process shown in these sketches. In the sketch above, water containing carbonic acid has seeped down through large cracks in porous limestone rock. At the water table under the limestone, the water eats its way horizontally, reaching a nearby river. Eventually the cave's ceiling collapses (*below*). By this time, the water table has been lowered. Water from the cave has spread into lower rocks and started to form a cave at the new level of the water table (*bottom*). The first cave is dry, except for rain water seeping down.

river. They are known as flood plains. During seasons of high water a river may overflow its banks, adding a fine layer of silt to the entire area.

If the layers of rock a young river cuts through are of different hardness, a cross section of the valley will look like a pair of staircases facing each other. In its Grand Canyon, the youthful Colorado River has been eroding this kind of staircase valley for 10 million years, producing the most striking landmark in the United States. In spots, the canyon is cut 6,000 feet into the Colorado Plateau. Since Lake Mead, downstream, is 2,000 feet lower than the upper canyon bed, it is clear that the Grand Canyon is destined to be dug a lot deeper in the next few million years.

When those last feet have been removed, the Colorado will no longer be a young river. Down-cutting will be at an end and the river will undertake a new project, side-cutting. Its side-to-side meanderings will mean eventual doom for every pinnacle, butte and mesa that now stand so spectacularly in the 12-mile gap between the north and south rims. Eventually, even the rims will be pushed back. Given enough time, and if there are no new upheavals in the region, the Grand Canyon of the distant future will consist of two lines of slanted bluffs with a 50-mile-wide flood plain between them. Through the plain, riding atop a thick blanket of its own sediments, will flow a gentle, elderly Colorado River.

Stripes of Ice and Earth

Like tributary streams that join to make a river, many glaciers creep out of their valleys to create a vast ribbon of ice, Barnard Glacier in Alaska. The dark stripes are moraines, composed of soil and rock that glaciers have collected along their edges as they plowed along the valley floors.

While streams run, glaciers merely crawl. Yet flowing ice can be one of the greatest forces of erosion. A glacier is an accumulation of snow that has slowly been compressed into ice. Eventually its weight gets so immense that it begins to flow downhill, gouging the bedrock in its path with stones and boulders embedded in its bottom, bulldozing soil and whatever else may be in the way. But a river goes as far in a few seconds as an average glacier does in a year. While some glaciers in Alaska advance as much as 40 feet in a day, many in the Alps creep downhill only a foot a day.

But it is not speed that accounts for a glacier's power. A glacier 1,000 feet thick exerts

a force of nearly 30 tons on each square foot on the valley floor underneath it, and the pressure enables the stones dragged along by the glacier to scour and polish the bedrock below. Valleys are begun by streams, but glacial erosion remodels the contours left by running water. The result is a U-shaped valley with a broad, flat floor and steep sides, strewn with rock debris deposited as the glacier recedes.

Until quite recently wind too was thought to be a major force of erosion. The weirdly balanced rocks, arches, spires, pinnacles and natural bridges of desert areas were all believed to have been shaped by the wind. Now geologists know that water was the

Pits from Rock on Rock

About 20,000 years ago, when mile-thick glaciers were moving across Canada, they gouged the underlying earth. Their tremendous pressure forced rocks frozen into the base of the ice against the ground, making ridges and grooves like these— some of which are a mile long and 200 feet deep.

71

principal agent, for wind must carry sand before it can cut, and even a strong wind cannot lift sand more than a few feet. Fine dust can be lifted much higher, but it is powerless to erode.

Natural arches and pinnacles often owe their shapes to mechanical weathering, a process that is noticeable in desert areas and that is helped by dry climate and wide swings in temperature. Sunlight plays a part in it: the dark-colored mineral grains in a granite block heat up faster than the lighter ones, and their different expansion rates bring on stresses that crumble the surface. Water, freezing in rock cracks and crevices, does more. It expands by 8 per cent when it freezes, acting like a crowbar in forcing the cracks apart. Similarly, in forest areas plant and tree roots do the same thing, penetrating the soil-filled fissures and splitting the rock simply by growing.

A great deal of weathering goes on underground, too. The raindrops that the earth soaks up fill the tiny spaces between soil and sand particles, penetrate the pores of rocks, and invade the earth's crust to a depth of hundreds of thousands of feet.

A Quiet Earth-Mover

This pretty little waterfall, spilling into a secluded pool, is actually part of Nature's greatest earth-mover—the mountain stream. Heavy vegetation like that seen here helps to hold the earth in place. But the swift-running water still washes stones and soil from the uplands, carving the rock as it goes.

There is more water underground at any one time than in all the lakes and rivers combined. When the water carries enough carbonic acid—from dissolved atmospheric carbon dioxide and from decaying organic material—chemical weathering occurs. The acid eats away at the rock, and the water becomes filled with dissolved limestone in the form of a calcium carbonate solution. In limestone flats the ground may collapse, producing the pits called sinkholes.

The same percolation process has hollowed out such earth cavities as Luray Cave in Virginia, Mammoth Cave in Kentucky, and the all but endless Carlsbad Caverns of New Mexico, with their many down-growing stalactites and up-growing stalagmites, columns and solid-rock veils, all made of calcium carbonate, precipitated drop by drop.

Weathering is vital to man, for its product of crumbled rock is the chief ingredient for soil, without which man could not grow the crops he needs in order to stay alive.

The sea is also an agent of erosion. Each year, every coast line on earth is worn away by the action of the tides. Yet the ocean can add to the landscape as well as take it away. The great sandspit called Cape Cod, for example, is being steadily devoured along its Atlantic Ocean beaches, but is being steadily rebuilt on the sheltered Cape Cod Bay side.

But the sea's prime function in the erosion cycle is to serve as a dumping ground for all the wastes of the land. The buildup of these deposits is concentrated on the continental shelves, spilling down the slope to depths of two or three thousand feet. Not much sediment from the land actually gets

A River Carves Its Course

As a river moves toward the sea, it begins to meander in a curving pattern, developing loops like those in the Yellowstone River shown at left. The water collides with the outer side of a curve, eroding the bank and picking up silt (*diagram, right*). Continuing downstream, the river drops this silt on inner curves. Thus one bank is cut away, one built up, and the river curves more sharply.

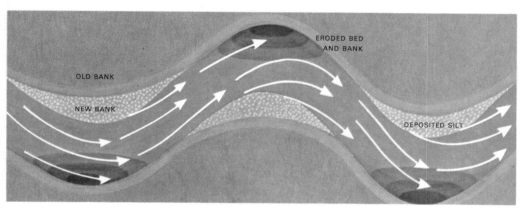

OLD BANK

NEW BANK

ERODED BED AND BANK

DEPOSITED SILT

to the deepest ocean bottoms. But at river deltas, most of which are underneath the water, tremendous burdens of sediments are borne by the sea floor and the underlying crust. The Piedmont district of Italy is composed of such stream deposits, and a similar plain stretches out from the western edge of the Sierra Nevada range in the United States. Nearly every river has a delta, except where the sea is deep or turbulent. The Mississippi's mud delta by now is perhaps 30,000 feet thick and nobody knows exactly how heavy. Some geologists think that parts of the gulf floor keep sinking as more sediment piles up.

As younger sediment deposits bury older ones, the older ones gradually are compressed into solid rock by the great weight above them. Gravel beds become a rock called conglomerate, sand becomes sandstone, clayey mud becomes shale, and calcite oozes turn into limestone. Even though most sediments end up in the ocean, the periodic upheavals of the crust along with changes of sea level during ice ages and thaws, have succeeded in leaving sedimentary rocks almost everywhere. About 80 per cent of the earth's surface is covered by them, though by far the greater part of the crust underneath still consists of igneous rock. Each major sedimentary rock has its own rate of deposition, an arbitrary measure based on the length of time it takes to build up a layer one foot thick. Although these rates can be estimated, they vary widely for each rock, depending on how favorable local conditions are. Shale, for example, may form at a rate of only one twentieth of an inch per thousand years—

or it may build up a layer nearly two feet thick in a thousand years.

By studying these sedimentary deposits, the geologist can unravel much of the history of erosion versus diastrophism. A limestone layer, whatever its present elevation above sea level, suggests that the region once formed the bed of a sea. A seam of coal indicates an ancient swamp whose rich vegetation was partly decomposed when it was inundated by water and buried under later rock. A layer of salt or gypsum points to a body of salt water that later dried up.

Sometimes the layers are all mixed up and the history takes some deciphering. One series of sedimentary layers may lie at an angle below the surface, and another series may lie horizontally above it. This is called an unconformity, and is good evidence that three geologic processes occurred there in a definite sequence. First, beds of sediment were uplifted, tilted and left above sea level by movements of the earth's crust. Second, erosion worked away at the uplifted strata until they were worn flat. Third, the region finally sank again below sea level, permitting more sediments to be deposited.

The Power of the Sea

These castlelike rocks off Scotland mark an older line of cliffs. The waves make such formations by attacking both sides of headlands that jut into the ocean. They may also punch out enormous archways in the rock; the tops of the arches eventually crumble, leaving their foundations standing alone.

SINKING INTO THE SEA, marshes along the South
Carolina coast are disappearing at the rate of a few
feet a century. About 100,000 years ago the area,
called the Pamlico Terrace, was high and dry, dotted
by low hills facing the ocean. All that is left of
the hills today is a series of small islands.

5

The Ever-moving
Ground beneath Us

The solid earth underfoot is not as solid as it seems. Actually it is undergoing constant stirrings. Sometimes these take place before our eyes, as when volcanoes spurt out molten rock or earthquakes wrack the globe's thin crust. But usually the shifts are on a far slower and larger scale, as whole regions rise or subside, tilt or warp, over millions of years. In fact we know now that continents move. They do so because the entire outer shell of the earth—the lithosphere—is broken up into plates that have shifted and changed shape over most of geologic history.

When we contemplate the earth's surface as we see it on a library globe, the striking feature about it is that most of the area—nearly three quarters—is drowned in ocean. Still more land would be submerged if the millions of cubic miles of ice that now smother polar and mountain areas were to melt and thus raise the sea level 200 to 300 feet. The continents of the earth are great plateaus of rock that project an average of about half a mile above the level of the sea.

Ordinary maps, which divide land from sea at the shoreline, do not give a true picture of continental outlines, for they fail to show the gently sloping floor that forms the natural continuation of most coastlines. These continental "shelves," as they are called, extend out to sea an average of 45 to 50 miles; some extend as far as 900 miles from the coastline. The outer edges of the shelves are considered the true limits of continents. After the shelves, the sea floor continues to slope downward, or drops sharply, to the huge, deep-ocean basins.

The ocean basins average two and a half miles in depth and possess as varied a terrain as do the continents. The largest mountain range on earth, in fact, is found below water. It stretches 47,000 miles through all the major ocean basins. The best known part, the Mid-Atlantic Ridge, runs for 12,000 miles from Iceland almost to Antarctica. Unseen by seafarers thousands of feet above, its peaks tower a mile or more above the sea floor. Mariners are familiar only with the few great mountains that thrust high enough to be visible as islands—the Azores, Ascension and Tristan de Cunha, among others. Isolated peaks called seamounts abound in oceanic basins, and long, narrow trenches—some deeper than Mount Everest is high—scar the basin floor here and there. However, for all this resemblance to the land, evidence indicates that the ocean floor not only differs quite markedly from the continents but also has a different history.

An additional basic fact about the earth's crust, whether above or below water, is that it is virtually all solid rock. This is not immediately apparent, for sediments cover the ocean floor and, on land, soil, vegetation and rock fragments such as sand and gravel are littered everywhere. But the cloak is only a few feet—or perhaps yards—thick, while the thickness of the underlying bedrock is measured in miles. Furthermore, the rocks at the surface are much the same as those throughout the earth's crust.

Rocks in the crust all belong to three great groups: the igneous, the sedimentary and the metamorphic. All igneous rocks were once molten and are believed to have come from deep in the earth, cooling at various rates and assuming various forms ranging from smooth basalt to grainy granite. Sedimentary rocks, as their name implies, are formed of layers of such materials as sand and clay that are washed down into lake beds and ocean floors. These sediments may be laid down by water, by ice or by wind. Cemented under pressure and often raised up again by later earth movements, they include sandstones and shales, limestones and dolomites. It is in these rocks, particularly in shales and limestones, that fossils are found. Metamorphic rocks are also aptly named: they are changed in form, reborn by heat and pressure during periods of deep burial. Thus slate was once clay, quartzite is a changed form of sandstone and marble began as limestone.

However they have been formed, rocks are complex mixtures of various elements in the form of mineral compounds. Of the 92 natural elements known on the earth, only eight are commonly involved in rock formations;

Currents Deep in the Earth

The outer shell of the earth, the lithosphere, is divided into plates that move away from mid-ocean ridges, where new sea floor is created, and dip down into the hot asthenosphere at trenches. Currents of heat, known as convection currents, circulate through the interior of the earth and rise at the mid-ocean ridges, bringing melted rock up to form new sea floor. The currents turn downward at the trench side of the plates, pulling the cold lithosphere down to melt in the asthenosphere.

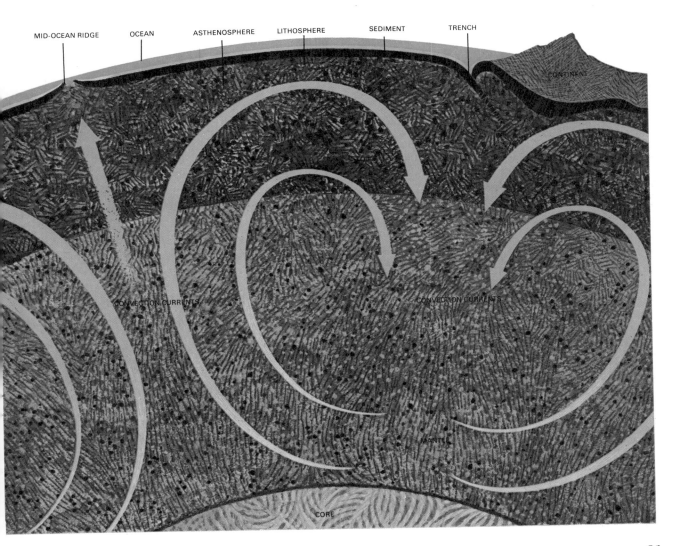

MID-OCEAN RIDGE   OCEAN   ASTHENOSPHERE   LITHOSPHERE   SEDIMENT   TRENCH

CONTINENT

CONVECTION CURRENTS   CONVECTION CURRENTS

MANTLE

CORE

Adrift on Plates of Rock

THE BIRTH OF THE CONTINENTS as we know them probably began about 200 million years ago. Before that, there was one land mass. Then it began to break up. The illustration at left shows the continents as they may have looked then, with Europe and Asia as one mass and all the rest of the continents bunched together in the other.

THE CONTINENTS TODAY are clearly separated. Antarctica has moved hundreds of miles due south, Australia is several thousand miles to the southeast, and North and South America are separated from Africa and Europe by the Atlantic Ocean. Africa, once connected to the Americas on its west coast, is now joined to Asia by the Middle East.

CONTINENTAL MOVEMENT may change the world map considerably in 30 million years. In this view, part of California, already moving northward at the rate of two inches a year, has become an island. Florida has linked with South America. Africa has drifted away again and the South Pacific islands and Australia are joining together.

they account for 98 per cent of the earth's crust by weight. The most abundant element in the crust—47 per cent of it—is oxygen. Silicon is next, at 28 per cent. From there the percentages fall off sharply: aluminum totals 8 per cent, iron 5 per cent, and sodium, magnesium, potassium and calcium each account for less than 4 per cent of the total. These eight common elements, together with several not-so-common ones, combine to form the nearly 2,000 known minerals. In terms of volume, compounds of oxygen and silicon predominate, and only a dozen or so mineral compounds account for the bulk of the earth's crust.

At the beginning of the 19th Century, the idea that there were three basic types of rock was still a new one. Geology at that time was a highly practical, applied science concerned chiefly with the mining of commercially important deposits of metals and other minerals. Nevertheless, there were those who went beyond the pick-and-shovel stage and speculated on how the rocks got there in the first place, and why there were so many kinds.

The theorists quickly found themselves in two rival groups. One group held that the earth had originally been covered with a thick sea and that everything now found in the crust—hard stones, soft stones, large and small stones, even fossils—was sediment that had been desposited by this sea. Because they took this view of the oceanic origin of the earth's crust, these men were known as Neptunists, after Neptune, the Greek god of

83

A Seabed in the Air

These weirdly twisted peaks in Montana are the work of two great earth-shaping processes. Millions of years ago, when an inland sea covered the area, layers of sediment were deposited, and slowly compressed by the weight of newer layers into rock. Finally there was a gigantic upheaval, which tipped and warped the layers to form this folded mountain.

84

the sea. Their opponents held that the principal factor in crust formation was the outpouring of volcanoes, past and present. For their support of fire, these theorists were known as Plutonists. Pluto, after whom they were named, was the ancient Greek god of the underworld.

Yet these two schools were arguing over only the small portion of the earth that could be inspected on the surface. The modern concept of the continents—that they are buoyant parts of the earth's lithosphere—was then unheard of. It had apparently occurred to nobody to wonder why the continents project upward the way they do.

On a world average, the continents protrude almost three miles above the ocean floors, and probably have since the beginning. What keeps these weighty continental blocks from sinking downward until they are level with the rest of the earth's crust?

The answer to this appears to be same as the answer to why a cork floats: in both cases, the bodies are buoyant because they are less dense than the material in which they are immersed. In the case of the continents, it is the lithosphere that plays the part of water, supporting the colossal corks, the continents. Granite is about 20 per cent lighter than the material beneath the continents. Basalt, on the other hand, is only 10 per cent lighter than the material beneath the oceans. The continents thus *must* ride higher than does the basaltic layer.

Another problem presents itself here. A cork does not float *on* water but *in* it. How far in is determined by a simple law discovered 2,200 years ago by Archimedes: if the cork weighs a pound, it will float just deep enough to displace a pound of water. In the same way, do the great blocks of granite that compose the continents have roots substantial enough for them actually to be floating like corks? Scientific investigation indicates that the continents indeed have massive roots that reach deep down to support the three miles or so that these blocks extend above the ocean floor.

A simplified model of the earth that is today used by many geophysicists in their calculations shows the continental blocks to be an average of 20 miles thick. The blocks are so heavy that they press the lithosphere down into the softer, underlying asthenosphere, thus making the latter's surface slightly dimpled.

The idea that a continent—or any major land mass, such as a large island—floats is illustrated by the fact that the entire Scandinavian peninsula has been rising. Pressed down by the weight of glaciers during the Ice Age, it has been rising ever since the glaciers departed 9,000 years ago. Scandinavia is now believed to stand nearly 1,000 feet higher than it did under the burden of the glaciers, and parts of it are now going up at the rate of three feet in every hundred years. Some estimates indicate that it still has about 650 feet to go.

The roots of continental blocks thrust

deep enough to dimple the underlying material—especially the roots of mountain ranges, which push down even deeper in order to support their weight, and to justify their greater height.

How continents came into being is one of the most difficult questions that one can ask about the earth. We assume that the first hard, or nearly hard, skin of the earth was formed more than four billion years ago by rocks left on the surface when heavier material in the original earth matter was pulled to the interior by gravity. When the processes of erosion and weathering began, sedimentary rock was added to blocks of land, and volcanic action continued to create rock. But how did these blocks become the continents we recognize today?

This brings up one of the most revolutionary concepts about the earth that has ever been proposed: the lithosphere, which is about 30 to 80 miles thick, is broken up into giant, shifting plates that collide, pull apart, or slide past one another—causing earthquakes in the process. The idea that plates slip along on the firm but plastic asthenosphere comes from an earlier theory proposing that continents shift their positions.

All through the 19th Century, scientists had asked themselves why it was that similar plants and animals were found on widely separated continents. A common explanation was the idea that there may have been land bridges that linked the various continents, but this idea was hard to accept: there

IGNEOUS ROCKS

OBSIDIAN

PUMICE

GRANITE

DIORITE

FISSURE FLOW

LAC

DIKE

SILL

BAT

Rocks Formed by Heat

Igneous rock begins as magma, or molten rock, far below the earth's surface. Many kinds of igneous rock cool and harden underground; the diagram below shows several forms such rock may take. If magma flows into fissures that are at an angle to the surrounding layers of rock, the resulting igneous rock is called a dike (*far left*). If magma flows parallel to the layers, the new rock is called a sill. Batholiths occur when magma forces its way through layers of existing rock; laccoliths force rock layers apart and make surface rock bulge. When molten rock does reach the surface it may merely flow from an opening, forming a fissure flow (a pool of rock) or a shield volcano. A violent volcano spews molten rock and gases; the lighter forms of igneous rock form a cone. At left are some of the most common igneous rocks. The first three in the bottom row were formed underground; the rest were formed on the surface.

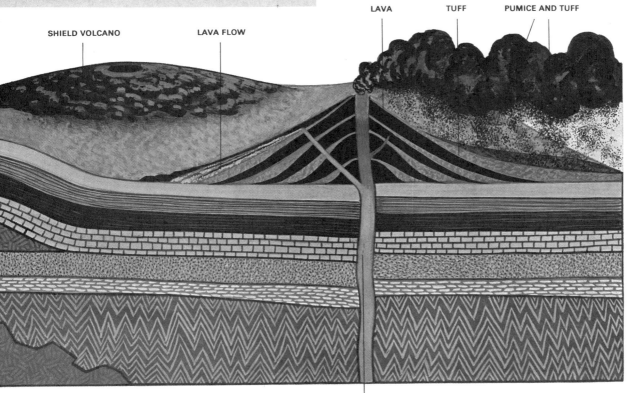

TUFF

RHYOLITE

GABBRO

BASALT

LAVA

TUFF

PUMICE AND TUFF

SHIELD VOLCANO

LAVA FLOW

CONDUIT

87

is no trace of most of the supposed bridges.

The possibility that continents moved was suggested by Alfred Wegener, a German meteorologist. Furthermore, he suggested that there once was a single, giant continental mass, and that the rest of the globe was covered by a single ocean. In time the huge continent, which he called Pangaea, cracked apart and the pieces wandered, to produce the continents of today.

This simple idea permitted Wegener to account for a number of odd facts besides the similarity in the patterns of evolution. For one thing, it suggested an explanation for why South Africa, India, Australia and part of South America bear the unmistakable scars of prehistoric glaciers and ice sheets. This is understandable if it is assumed that these lands once surrounded the South Pole, which Wegener believed had been near the west coast of Africa. Similarly, the coal deposits of Europe, North America and Antarctica suggest that these continents were probably near the equator in the past. Merely glancing at a globe seems to verify continental drift: the coastline of the Americas closely matches that of western Europe and Africa, as if the two had actually been torn apart at some time in the past. There are even matching rock formations in Norway and Canada in the north, and in South Africa and South America in the south.

Although the theory of continental drift was long dismissed, geologists became interested in it again after the Second World War when scientists began to map the ocean floors and to study earthquake waves with new, advanced instruments. The long, snaky Mid-Atlantic Ridge not only showed up clearly on the maps but also proved to be the site of many of the earthquakes that were constantly recorded.

Further mapping of the oceans revealed additional mountain ridges in the ocean basin; and again, earthquakes were pinpointed where the ridges were. Little by little, an explanation for the seeming coincidence began to take shape. Earthquakes marked places where the ocean floor was spreading apart. Such action could, in turn, explain how the huge land mass, Pangaea, had broken up to become individual continents.

There was also another way of determining whether or not the continents had shifted— by studying the magnetism of rocks. Since mineral grains in rocks become magnetized in the direction of the earth's magnetic field at the time the rocks are hardening, the fact that many such polarized rocks in the continents had their magnetic fields pointing in different directions suggested either that the poles had moved, or that the rocks had.

There are good theoretical reasons for believing that the magnetic and geographic poles, while they are known to move somewhat, relative to each other, do not ever vary by more than about 10 or 12 degrees. Therefore, any polarized rocks pointing farther than that from the magnetic north can be assumed to have moved—or the continents in which they lie may have moved. The evi-

Rocks Made by Pressure

As soon as a mountain is built, water and ice begin tearing it down. Water seeps into cracks, expands as it freezes, and breaks off large chunks, which form rock slumps. A glacier picks up rock and dirt, depositing them in a pile, or moraine. Mountain streams deposit sediment in an alluvial fan. The streams drop the largest rocks first, to form breccia. Smaller bits are deposited downstream and eventually turn to sandstone, while the tiniest particles of clay are carried to the river's end and are compressed into shale. All sedimentary rocks are formed by the pressure exerted by newer layers of sediment upon the old. Swamp vegetation trapped in these layers turns to coal. Minerals from coral reefs are dissolved by the ocean, then deposited on the sea floor to become limestone.

SEDIMENTARY ROCKS

BRECCIA

CONGLOMERATE

SANDSTONE

BITUMINOUS (SOFT) COAL

SHALE

LIMESTONE

COQUINA

GYPSUM

TRAVERTINE

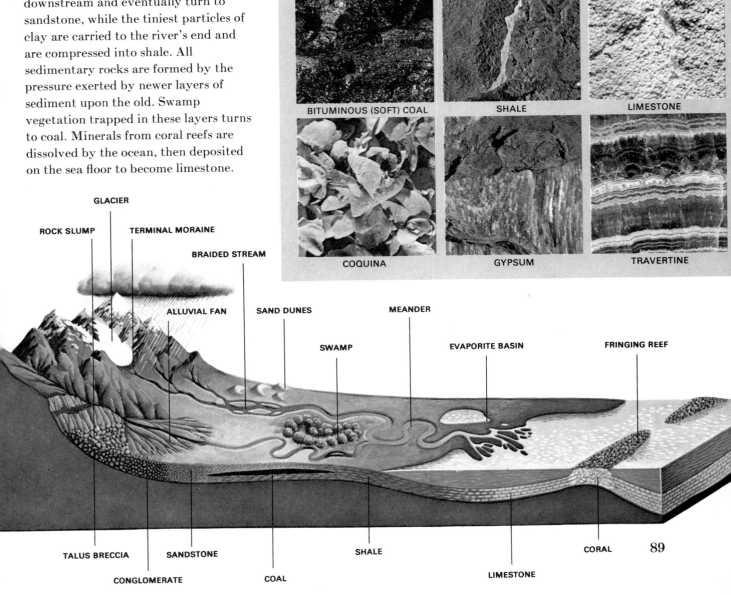

GLACIER

ROCK SLUMP

TERMINAL MORAINE

BRAIDED STREAM

ALLUVIAL FAN

SAND DUNES

MEANDER

SWAMP

EVAPORITE BASIN

FRINGING REEF

TALUS BRECCIA

SANDSTONE

CONGLOMERATE

COAL

SHALE

LIMESTONE

CORAL

89

SOME METAMORPHIC AND SEDIMENTARY ROCKS

LIMESTONE

MARBLE

SANDSTONE

QUARTZITE

SHALE

SLATE

SCHIST

GNEISS

GRANITE

Rocks That Change

Under intense heat and pressure, sedimentary rock can be changed into the third basic type of rock, metamorphic (from the Greek for "changed"). How this happens is shown in the cutaway drawing below. At far left, molten granite has forced its way into contact with layers of limestone, sandstone and shale. Although the heat is not enough to melt the rocks, it does alter their structure: limestone becomes marble, sandstone turns to quartzite and shale is changed to hornfels, a type of slate. At the right is shown the effect of great pressure and temperature caused by buckling in the earth's crust. Shale undergoes a succession of changes, and may end up as a form of granite. The photographs at left include the major sedimentary rocks (limestone, sandstone and shale) and the metamorphic rocks they can become.

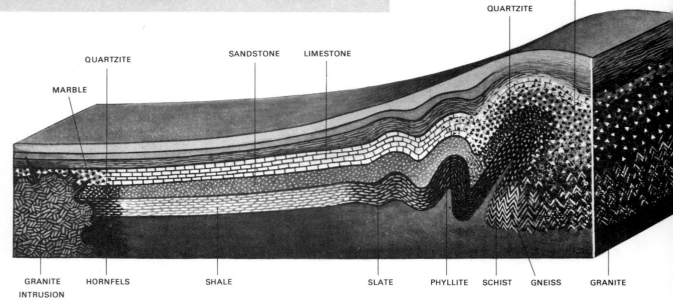

MARBLE

QUARTZITE

SANDSTONE   LIMESTONE

QUARTZITE

MARBLE

GRANITE
INTRUSION   HORNFELS   SHALE   SLATE   PHYLLITE   SCHIST   GNEISS   GRANITE

dence does indicate some continental drift.

As it turned out, studying the magnetism of rocks contributed more than support for the theory of continental drift. It also provided a way to prove that the sea floor did, and does, spread. Using submersible instruments that measure magnetism, scientists found matching ribbons of rock that stretched across the ocean floor on either side of the mid-ocean ridges. Each ribbon recorded magnetic reversals, caused by changes in the direction of the magnetic field at the time the rock-producing magma rose to the sea floor from deep within the earth.

The molten stuff that rises at the mid-ocean ridges and erupts from volcanoes above ground is called magma when it is underground and lava when it emerges. The nature of a volcanic eruption depends upon the composition of the rock and the amount of gas and water it contains. A thick, slow-flowing magma, laden with gas, tends to escape explosively, spewing fragments of solidified lava and clouds of steam and hot gases. A thinner magma, with lower gas content, pushes out in quieter fashion, forming tongues of white-hot lava that creep downhill until they harden.

The giant volcanoes that have formed the Hawaiian Islands rear as high as 30,000 feet above the ocean floor and about 14,000 feet above sea level. They are thought to be surface signs of hot spots that exist in the asthenosphere, or perhaps even deeper in the mantle. Lava from the active volcanoes of Hawaii often emerges as a glowing, highly fluid stream, sometimes spurting up in fountains when a pocket of gas comes to the surface. Such flows may travel far before solidifying; they produce wide-based mountains. Volcanoes with thick lavas, on the other hand, build up steep, narrow cones.

Magma is always the product of plate movement, but it does not always reach the surface, either at mid-ocean ridges or in volcanoes. If it can find no outlet or if there is not enough pressure behind it to force one, it may merely thrust its way up into cracks or between layers of rock near the surface. Sometimes it forms underground pockets, pushing up the surface above it like a blister but not breaking through. Often it runs along natural fissures, occasionally engulfing and melting what lies in its path.

Magma that has worked its way into a crack that runs at an angle to the surrounding layers of rock and has subsequently hardened there is called a dike. Dikes vary in width from a few inches to several yards and may be many miles in length. They may be revealed millions of years after their formation when the softer rock around them has been eroded away, leaving the dikes exposed to the elements, running like long fences across the surface of the land. A few dikes are immense. One in Rhodesia is 300 miles long and as much as five miles wide.

A sheet of solidified magma that runs parallel to the layers of rock around it is known as a sill. The magnificent cliffs known as the

(Text continued on page 94)

CHALCANTHITE

GARNET

CHRYSOTILE (ASBESTOS)

AMETHYST

VARISCITE

A spectacular display, from fragile fibers to gleaming gems, suggests the

YELLOW WULFENITE

BOTRYOIDAL, AZURITE, MALACHITE, LIMONITE

MICROCLINE, SMOKY QUARTZ

RUBY SPHALERITE

PYRITE, QUARTZ

eat variety among the 2,000-odd minerals found in the earth's crust.

Diamonds From the Deep

Diamond, the hardest natural material, is thought to be made some 240 miles below the earth's surface, where temperatures are at least 5,000° F. and pressures are over a million pounds per square inch. After diamonds have cooled, they form a plug in the crust. Eventually they become exposed because the rock above has eroded. One plug in South Africa, now mined and abandoned (*left*), produced $188 million worth of diamonds in 26 years. Below is a rough diamond found in South Africa. At right is a pan of gemstones, which have been washed in acid. They are worth about three quarters of a million dollars.

Palisades that line the bank of the Hudson River across from New York City are in reality a tremendous sill. The most gigantic of all molten rock formations are batholiths, which may extend tens of thousands of square miles, deep into the lithosphere.

The texture and appearance of magma vary enormously according to whether the magma has been cooled rapidly on the surface of the earth in the form of lava or whether it has remained underground in batholiths and cooled very slowly. The rapid cooling of lava gives it a fine-grained character ranging all the way from obsidian, which is the most

quickly cooled of all lava and looks like blackish glass, to basalt, a smooth, dark, dense material that is the most common of all volcanic rocks. Underground magma cools so slowly that its structure is much coarser. Dikes are mostly basalt and batholiths are made of granitic rock, which is a grainy rock, speckled in color and full of relatively large particles of different minerals.

Batholiths—and a great many volcanoes —are formed where lithospheric plates meet head on. In such collisions, the edge of one plate dips down under the other and dives into the hot asthenosphere, creating a trench where it plunges. As the cold, rigid

slab works its way into the hot material, it begins to melt itself as well as to squeeze the rock between it and the plate above. Both melting and squeezing produce magma, which either cools underground or erupts on the surface in volcanic activity.

The outer shell of the earth is made up of at least six large plates and six smaller ones. They move at various speeds, in different directions. The huge plate that carries Europe and Asia, for example, is scarcely moving at all. What little movement there is, is eastward. By comparison, the Pacific plate is hurrying along to the west and north, plunging down into many different trenches. It dips under the Eurasian plate in the northwest near the Kurile Islands, the North American plate at the Aleutians, the Philippine plate near the Mariana Islands and the Indian plate around New Zealand.

In a collision, an oceanic plate is no match for a plate carrying a continent. The ocean plate is forced under because it is thinner and also because its basaltic rock is heavier —and hence less buoyant—than the granitic rock in a continent. However, sedimentary rock on an ocean floor is lighter than basalt too. For this reason, very little of it is ever dragged down into a trench. When an oceanic plate and a continent meet, the sediment of the ocean floor is gathered and pushed up to form mountains. The Andes in South America are a good example of mountains that are formed in this manner.

There is also another kind of plate collision. Sometimes one continent bumps into another one. This, too, creates rugged mountains as one continental mass grinds under the other. The Himalayas were formed by this process about 40 million years ago, when part of the Indian plate ploughed into Asia. India had once nestled close to Africa and Antarctica in Pangaea, but as the supercontinent broke up, the Indian plate drifted away to the north and east. Even after the section carrying India ran into Asia, it continued to move north, ramming its way under the more massive continent. Its action not only raised the mountain range but also uplifted the volcano-studded Tibetan plateau behind it. To this day, the Indian plate is still pushing north under the Eurasian plate—and the Himalayas are still rising.

What force, we must ask, is powerful enough to propel the great plates and so dramatically affect the geography of the earth? No one knows for sure, although scientists have offered several possible explanations. The internal heat of the earth may well be responsible. Most scientists believe that hot currents circulate through the asthenosphere, rising at the ocean ridges, spreading horizontally under the bottom of the plates and pulling down the cold lithospheric slabs at trenches. There may also be small, localized currents as well as large ones.

Perhaps heat propels the lithospheric plates in another way. Some scientists feel that hot spots, like those that are believed to have created the Hawaiian Islands, coax plates into motion by their eruptions.

Still another theory argues that gravity controls plate action. Since plates are highest at the ridges where magma surges up to form new crust, their slight tilt may cause the ocean floor to slide down from the height of a ridge to a trench.

Whatever creates plate movement, we can be sure it has gone on for a long time. In fact, it is possible the lithosphere has been broken into plates for four billion years—ever since it became cold and rigid enough to be cracked by uncontainable forces bursting from within our dynamic earth.

Prospecting for Uranium

Using a Geiger counter, a prospector searches over a vein of yellow carnotite. This material, found mostly in the Colorado Plateau, is a major source of uranium in the United States. When the metal is purified, it becomes the fuel for nuclear reactors, as well as the basic ingredient for nuclear bombs.

6

A Record of Life
in the Rocks

How old is the earth? One way of measuring its age is to determine the age of the rocks of the earth's crust, many of which have existed for millions and millions of years. The study of ancient layers of rock has told scientists many things, not only about age, but about evolution and the conditions of climate that existed in the distant past.

One measuring stick that is used is radioactive dating. A radioactive element is useful because it has a precise rate of decay. Atom by atom, it turns into a more stable element. Radioactive carbon, known as carbon-14, loses exactly half its store of radioactivity in 5,730 years by conversion into nitrogen. A specialist with delicate measuring instruments can compare the amount of radioactive carbon remaining in a fossil with the amount of ordinary carbon, and in that way calculate how old the fossil is. For in the first 5,730 years the amount of radioactive carbon will drop by one half and in the next 5,730 years by another half, and so on until none remains.

Radioactive carbon is a superb tool for the prehistorian. But it is less useful for the geologist, who is concerned for the most

DRILLING FOR BONES, workmen clear rock away from a dinosaur skeleton at the Dinosaur National Monument in Utah. The bulk of the rock is broken away with the drill, and the bones are freed with delicate tools. Discovering such bones tells us much about animals that lived before man existed.

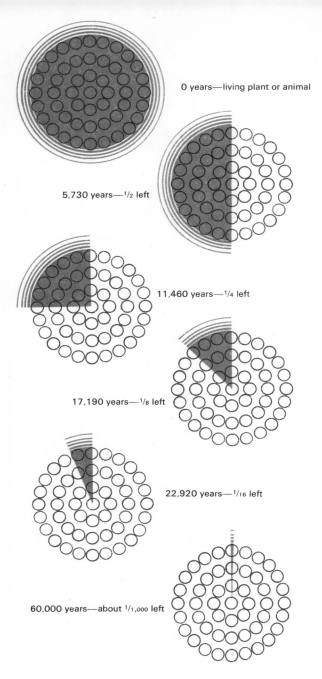

0 years—living plant or animal

5,730 years—½ left

11,460 years—¼ left

17,190 years—⅛ left

22,920 years—1/16 left

60,000 years—about 1/1,000 left

A Way of Measuring Age

These diagrams illustrate what is called the "carbon 14" method of telling a fossil's age. The tissues formed by living organisms have radioactive carbon 14 as one of their basic components. Over long periods of time, this carbon 14 decays into nitrogen. Half decays every 5,730 years, as shown above. By measuring the amount of carbon 14 that is left in a fossil the scientist can calculate its age.

part with periods of time vastly longer than its rather short half-life. He must find radioactive materials with half-lives of millions or billions of years. Luckily, they exist. An isotope of potassium decays into argon with a half-life of 1.3 billion years; an isotope of thorium decays into lead with a half-life of 14 billion years, and an isotope of rubidium decays into strontium with a half-life of 60 billion years.

A particularly useful radioactive tool for geologists is uranium. Traces of uranium are found in many rocks and in widely scattered areas on the earth's surface. All uranium on earth will eventually become lead. However, this takes place with fantastic slowness. At the end of 2.25 billion years, three fourths of an original chunk of an isotope of uranium will still be uranium, and one fourth will have turned to lead.

The oldest known rocks today are found in Europe, Greenland and Labrador. They are all close to four billion years old. Even the four-billion-year figure leaves open the question of how much older the earth is than its oldest rocks. However, the principle of radioactive dating can be applied to this problem in a most ingenious way. Recently such studies have been made of the fragments of meteorites, giving age estimates of about 4.5 billion years. Meteors are, like the earth, part of the solar system. Since it is generally assumed that all of the solar system came into existence at the same time, most geologists believe that the earth is the same age as the meteorites.

We toss millions and billions about very glibly. Yet they are such staggeringly large units of time that it is worth pausing to try to emphasize just how long 4.5 billion years really is. Hendrik Van Loon did it with this fanciful opening to his famous book, *The Story of Mankind:*

"High up in the North in the land called Svithjod, there stands a rock. It is a hundred miles high and a hundred miles wide. Once every thousand years a little bird comes to this rock to sharpen its beak.

"When the rock has thus been worn away, then a single day of eternity will have gone by."

A less dramatic but perhaps more useful way of emphasizing the age of the earth is to compare it with the evolution of man. It is generally believed that human beings have evolved during the last two million years. The earth on which they evolved is more than 2,000 times that old.

What is known about the slow process that first brought life into existence on the earth? So far, almost nothing. Biochemists and physicists believe that the earth's early atmosphere and oceans contained the raw materials for the formation of protein molecules. Recent studies have indicated that the chemical broth in the ancient oceans could have been organized into amino acids through the action of lightning. Amino acids have been turned into protein molecules in the laboratory; from this all else could follow. The major requirement is time. It is

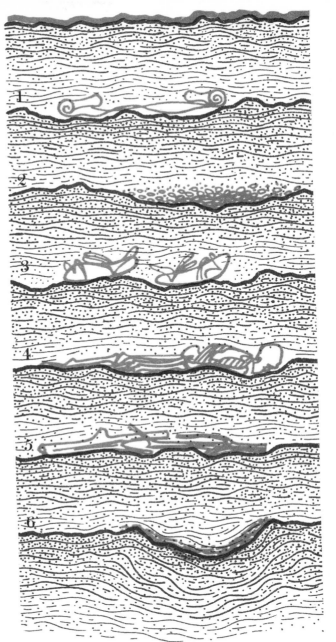

Some Fossil Treasures

Objects dated by the carbon 14 method are shown above. It proved the famous Dead Sea Scrolls (*1*) to be at least 1,900 years old. Some Japanese lotus seeds (*2*) were found to be 3,000 years old. Sandals (*3*) in an Oregon cave were dated at 9,000 years, objects near a skeleton in Illinois (*4*) at 10,000 years. A Wisconsin tree (*5*) died 11,000 years ago. Charcoal found in Iraq (*6*) kept men warm in 30,000 B.C.

101

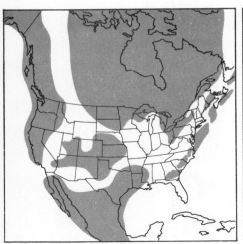

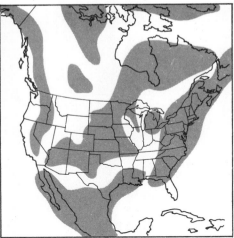

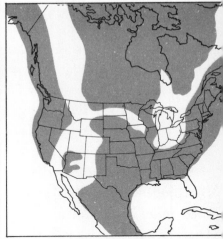

CAMBRIAN PERIOD   ORDOVICIAN PERIOD   DEVONIAN PERIOD

Where the Sea Used to Be

At various times long ago, North America was covered by
the sea. In the Cambrian period the sea (white) reached
over much of the United States. In the Ordovician period
the sea was even more extensive. By the late Devonian the
land had made gains. The sea kept retreating, though in
Carboniferous times most of the West was an ocean and in
the Cretaceous period water reached into Canada. Not until
the Miocene did the present continent almost entirely emerge.

CARBONIFEROUS PERIOD   CRETACEOUS PERIOD   MIOCENE PERIOD

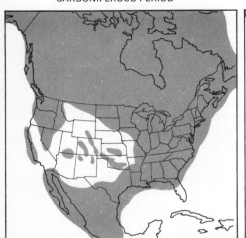

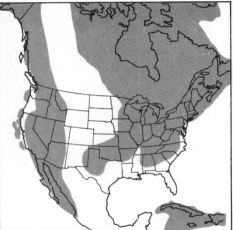

estimated that the change from simple organic compounds to the earliest one-celled organism may well have taken one third as long as the later development from one-celled animal to man. The fossil record shows not only that time was available, but that life did get under way very slowly.

Geologists divide earth history into two periods, called eons. The first, and by far the larger one, is known as the Cryptozoic eon, from the Greek for "hidden life." It covers the time from the earliest known rocks up to some 600 million years ago, a span of about 3.3 billion years. The second, or Phanerozoic eon—from the Greek for "visible life"—extends to today.

Rocks from the Cryptozoic eon occur where the cores of ancient mountain systems have been laid bare by erosion or where deep gorges have been cut into high plateaus. These ancient outcrops, which are called shields, constitute an enormous amount of material and are found in many spots on the earth's surface. The fossils that have so far been discovered in them consist of many kinds of algae, bacteria and plants, fragments of a wormlike animal, and soft-bodied animals that look like jellyfish.

This seems a pitifully small harvest from more than three billion years of earth history. However, it may not be the entire story. Cryptozoic animals were all water dwellers, and apparently did not develop any hard parts such as shell, cartilage or bone. There may have been many more of them, and a greater variety, than the Cryptozoic rocks show. Some Cryptozoic rocks are rich in organic carbon, and this could represent the last traces of living things. Nonetheless, there is a startling contrast between life on earth during the Cryptozoic eon—even at the end of that eon—and life during the earliest Phanerozoic.

There are three great subdivisions of the Phanerozoic eon, known as eras. First comes the Paleozoic era (ancient life), then the Mesozoic era (in-between life), and finally the Cenozoic era (recent life). The Paleozoic era, which lasted 375 million years, came to a close 225 million years ago. The Mesozoic lasted for 155 million years. The Cenozoic, the era in which we live, began only 70 million years ago.

Just as eons are broken up into eras, so eras are divided into periods. The earth at the start of the Paleozoic's first period, the Cambrian, was somewhat different from what it is today. The sea was probably larger than it is now. The continents were slightly lower and smaller than they are today. The rocks were bare of plant life except for lichens and a handful of other very primitive plants. There were no animals on land at all. The general atmosphere was one of mildness and calm—and apparent agelessness, for the Cambrian period went on and on in this manner for 100 million years.

In the sea, however, things were much livelier. The progression from simple organic compounds to single-celled organisms, and from there to multicelled forms, had now reached the point where the sea was swarming with a variety of creatures, some of them weighing as much as 10 pounds.

The outstanding living form of the Cambrian period was the trilobite. It was the great evolutionary triumph of its time, the most efficient creature the world had ever seen. It was sort of a cross between a horseshoe crab and a clawless lobster, with a shell and numerous spindly legs. Its segmented body also allowed it to roll up into a tight ball for defense. Trilobites developed a wide variety of shapes and sizes, and were much more advanced than anything else of their day. And their day was a long one; it lasted more than 300 million years.

The Cambrian period was followed by the Ordovician. This period was marked by considerable geologic disturbance. For a time the oceans divided what would become North America into a group of islands, and mountains in New England began to rise. In the seas trilobites continued in enormous throngs. The Ordovician also saw the appearance of the first animal with a backbone. It was only a primitive, jawless fish, but it *did* have a backbone, and is the oldest of its kind that has been found.

The following period, the Silurian, lasted a mere 40 million years. During the Silurian, part of the eastern United States was slowly transformed by coastal uplift into a landlocked inland sea, which gradually evaporated, leaving an immense salt desert. These salt deposits have been extensively mined in

A History of Life on Earth

The length of time that life has been evolving is shown here in two different ways. Below, the time since the earth began, at least 4.5 billion years, is represented by a spiral measuring tape. Life began less than a quarter of the way up the tape, and man developed only near the very top. At right is a diagram of the Grand Canyon and the fossils that have been found there. Here evolution's history is beautifully laid out. The Colorado River has cut through layer after layer of sedimentary rock, exposing fossils of many different periods. In the bottom layer are fossils of algae, tiny sea plants that are among the earliest types of life. Higher layers contain more complex forms of life; scorpion and starfish remains are common in the layer deposited in Cambrian times. At the top of the canyon, in the Permian layers, are more modern trees and insects.

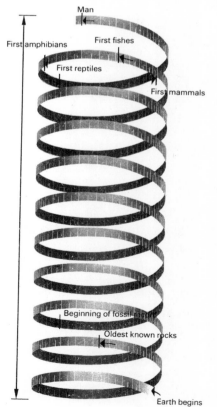

Man
First amphibians
First fishes
First reptiles
First mammals
Beginning of fossils
Oldest known rocks
Earth begins

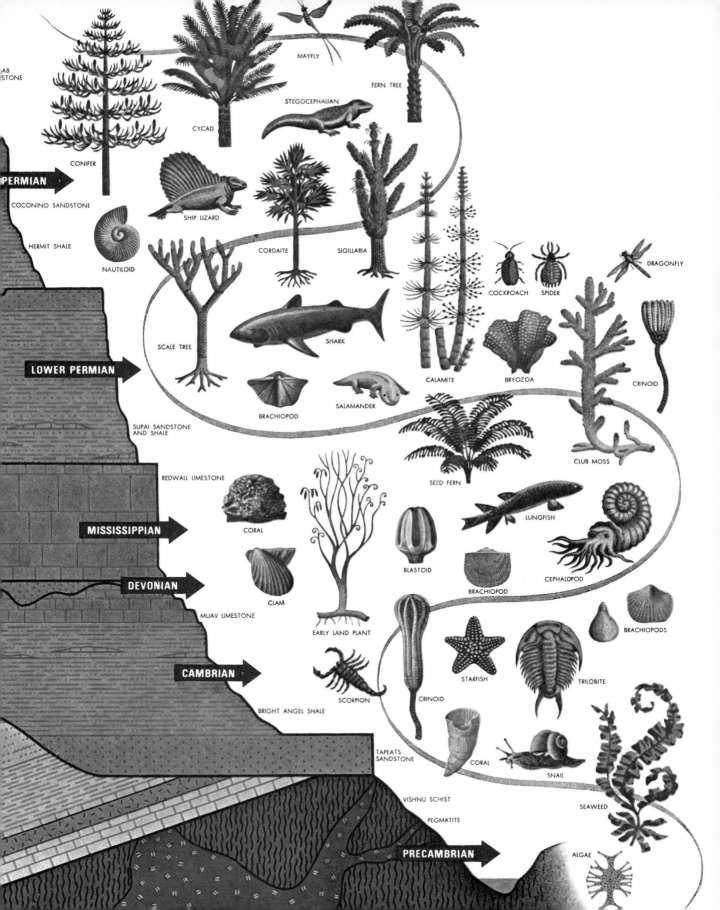

New York, Pennsylvania and Michigan. Altogether, the dry salt lake may have extended over 100,000 square miles.

Life in the warm oceans continued to increase in numbers. The durable trilobite lingered on, but in modified form. Many now were covered with spines, presumably as a protection against the superior mobility of the evolving fish. Corals were very common. A gigantic water scorpion appeared, its nine-foot length an all-time record for its kind. This immense scorpion completely overshadowed a little-known relative, which was only about two inches long, but which was to be infinitely more important to the overall course of evolution. For this small creature, along with an equally inconspicuous spider, shares the honor of being the first animal to venture on dry land.

In the next age, the Devonian period, 18 different kinds of spiders lived on land along with a wingless insect. Fish continued to develop, but the most important ones were those that were destined to become the ancestor of frogs and salamanders. These fishes, named Crossopterygii, had a primitive set of lungs, which they used to breathe air, and strong, stumpy fins, with which they could "walk" on land.

Land plants also developed in the Devonian and continued during the next period, the Carboniferous, which began 350 million years ago and lasted about 80 million years. It was a time of minor geologic activity. On land there were vast forest swamps choked

The Remains of Ancient Life

Ancient animals and plants are sometimes preserved in the form of fossils like those shown here. When a plant or animal dies it usually decays, but if it falls into a soft material such as clay, which later hardens, it may leave a perfect print (right). Sometimes a whole leaf can be preserved, when minerals enter the cells and harden there, as they did in the leaf at top right. With animals, usually only the bones are preserved, as in the case of the tree climbing Uintacyon (center right). A fly's entire skeleton, preserved in amber, is shown below.

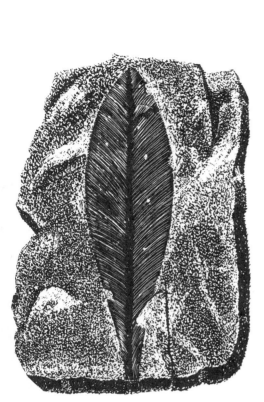

FERN LEAF

PLATANUS LEAF

UINTACYON

FLY

with plants and trees. These were buried in water over and over again across huge expanses of the earth's surface. Bedded down in mud, crushed by pressures from the sediments piling up above them, these forgotten forests were compressed into some of the world's great coal deposits, which give the Carboniferous period its name.

Many insects developed during the Carboniferous, including one that resembled a dragonfly but had a wingspread of two and a half feet. With them came the first traces of a new group of vertebrates, the reptiles. These were the first backboned animals to free themselves completely from the water. Amphibians must return to water to mate and lay their fragile eggs; their young, just as the tadpoles of frogs still do, must pass through a free-swimming aquatic state before they can return to land in mature form. The great innovation supplied by the reptiles was that their eggs had tough cases and could be deposited anywhere without being in danger of drying up, and their young could start living on land the moment they were hatched. This final liberation from the sea ranks as a major event in the history of life.

The last of the Paleozoic periods, the Permian, was a time of active mountain-building, and for the first time in hundreds of millions of years there was a drastic change in the climate. The Permian experienced severe ice ages, which covered parts of Africa, Australia and South America with glaciers.

Other parts of the world turned to deserts. Drying seas produced the three largest salt deposits in the world, one in Russia, one in Germany and one stretching from Kansas to New Mexico in the United States. Altogether, this was a very difficult period for life.

The denizens of the Carboniferous swamps, both plant and animal, were ill-fitted to withstand the cold and extreme dryness. Many of them died out during this time. Reptiles adapted well, but in the sea the trilobites finally reached the end of the line. At last it became extinct.

Thus ended the Paleozoic. The period that followed, the Mesozoic, lasted 155 million years. During the Mesozoic, reptiles became the dominant type of animal and, as the period wore on, they grew in both number and size. Some of them returned to the sea in the form of dolphin-like animals with long, toothed snouts. Others wallowed in the swamps, munching enormous quantities of the marsh and river plants there. By the middle of the period, these reptiles had evolved into the largest land animals the world has ever known.

This was the age of dinosaurs. Among their number was Diplodocus, a "typical" dinosaur with a long neck, a tiny head containing an even tiner brain, a large body, huge legs and a long tail. Diplodocus was 90 feet long. A tanklike animal called Stegosaurus went lumbering through the woods, its back protected by huge, bony plates set on edge, and its tail armed with three-foot spikes. Stego-

Life's Beginnings

Life on earth probably began in very simple form. Dr. Stanley Miller (*center picture*) has conducted experiments showing how certain chemicals basic to living organisms could have formed when the earth was young. Although we have no record of this occurrence, we do have fossils of very ancient and very simple forms of life. The top picture shows a fossil one-celled bacterium three billion years old; at the bottom is a fossil of a rod-shaped bacterium two billion years old.

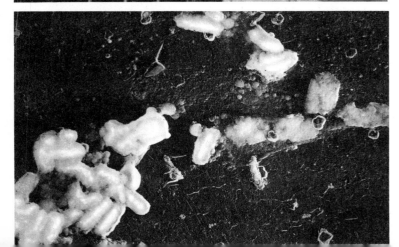

saurus was a slow-moving and even slower-witted creature, with a two-and-a-half-ounce brain housed in a 10-ton body.

Another group of dinosaurs were meat eaters. Agile and hungry, they ran along on their hind legs, dangling small forelegs as they went. Some were no larger than chickens. Others, like Allosaurus and Tyrannosaurus were undoubtedly the most fearsome animals ever known, and preyed on the huge, inoffensive plant eaters. Meanwhile, relatives of the dinosaurs took to the air, gliding over the sea on leathery wings with a spread of some 50 feet. These were not birds, nor were they bats. They were flying reptiles with small bodies and thin, hollow bones.

Although the Mesozoic period was dominated by reptiles, the first birds appeared then, as did the first mammals. Birds and mammals are both warm-blooded, and this gives them an immense advantage over insects, amphibians and reptiles.

All cold-blooded animals, if it gets too hot, suffer heat prostration. A small lizard living in burning desert sands must scamper quickly from one patch of shade to another, or it will die in a few minutes. It is only the bird or mammal, gasping or sweating to cool its body, that can stay out in the hot sun for long periods of time. Similarly, when the temperature falls, a cold-blooded animal becomes motionless.

Mammals, having the ability to produce their own body heat, and with fur outside and a layer of fat just beneath the skin to help retain the heat, can stand extremes of cold almost indefinitely. On the other hand, they require a steady supply of food in order to keep their internal furnaces stoked; the extreme example is the shrew, which must eat heartily every hour or two, or it will starve to death. By contrast, a cold-blooded python needs a good meal only about once a year. During our era, the Cenozoic, warm-blooded animals have become dominant.

Man, the most advanced mammal, has now evolved to the point where he can reason, remember, read and write, and devise scientific instruments and laboratories. Out of all this comes the momentous discovery that there is such a thing as evolution. Then, out of that discovery comes the science of genetics—and with it the key to the shaping of the further course of evolution.

A Rare Fossil Find

A beautifully preserved fossil, this fish is called *Mene rhombeus*, and it is a relative of the modern pompano. Fifty million years ago it swam in the seas off Italy. Such fossils are extremely valuable to paleontologists, for it is rare to find one like this in which every bone and fin is still easy to see.

7
The Uncertain Future of the Earth

A FROZEN EARTH, pictured about 50 billion years from now, can support no life as we know it. The moon may have drawn closer to the earth and the sun will be only a flicker. Man will have been extinct for a long time—unless he has found a way to move the human race to another planet.

No oracle of ancient times ever performed such impressive predictions as today's scientist does when he foretells the swaying of an unbuilt skyscraper in a hurricane, the spiraling orbits of an unlaunched astronaut or the power of an unexploded nuclear bomb. Yet these feats are child's play compared with the attempts of modern earth theorists to forecast the trends taking place in the land, sea and air of man's planet. Scientists hope and expect that their crystal balls will not always be so cloudy. Meteorologists, armed with computers, are already calculating day-to-day weather on the basis of mathematical models of the entire atmosphere. They are increasingly able to improve their results as they learn to use the information from orbiting weather satellites. Eventually they hope to understand long-term climates as well as short-term weather—to look months, years and perhaps even centuries into the future and predict worldwide changes in temperature, ocean level and movements of glaciers. If they are successful and can learn to forecast floods and famines well ahead of time, it will permit nations to forearm themselves

The Fate of the Moon

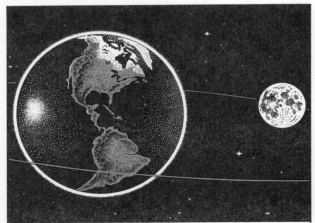

THE MOON'S POSSIBLE FUTURE is shown in these drawings. Above, the moon is seen in its present orbit, one that grows larger as the earth, spinning more slowly, exerts less pull on it.

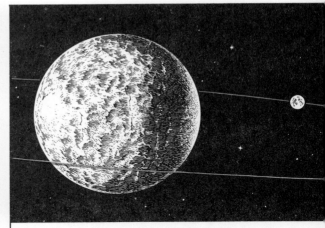

SPIRALING INTO SPACE, the moon continues to increase the size of its orbit as the earth's rotation continues to slow. Eventually one day on earth will be as long as a month is today.

against natural disasters and perhaps even to participate in international weather-control programs.

Since weather is vitally important to trade and commerce, it has been studied more intensively than most earth processes. But a small, hard-working group of earth scientists is also busy measuring and analyzing the other forces of change that mold the earth's future. Hardly a month goes by in which some scientist somewhere does not find evidence with which to improve or refine the explanation of some earthly phenomenon. Sir Isaac Newton explained the oceans' tides; today's physicists have added tides raised in the atmosphere by both moon and sun, an even land tides four or six inches high, raised in the solid rock of the earth's crust. To the earth's simple rotation they have added wobbles and nods. To visible sunlight and starlight they have added a whole spectrum of cosmic energy: radio waves, infrared waves, ultraviolet waves, X-rays and gamma rays, and even tiny bits of matter that come cannon-balling toward earth from stars that exploded long ago in the depths of space.

It may take decades to fit together all the puzzling pieces of evidence into a true portrait of the earth. No other field of science encompasses such a wealth of unexplained facts. For example, there is the fact that the ocean levels in the Northern Hemisphere drop eight inches every spring. There should be a compensating rise in the oceans south of the equator, but there is none. No one knows where the water goes. Mapmaking reveals

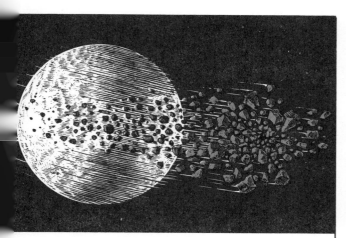

RETURNING TO EARTH, the moon responds to the earth's pull again when the earth day becomes longer than a month. If it comes too close, the earth's gravitational pull may shatter it.

A RING AROUND THE EARTH will be formed if the moon does break up. Observed from far away, the earth would then resemble the solar system's other ringed planets, Saturn and Neptune.

other problems. Until as recently as 1948 the local curvature of the earth in Europe was so little known that the maps of different countries did not join properly. Maps that had been made in Sweden differed from maps in Denmark by 300 feet. English and French maps were out of mesh by 600 feet.

The Ice Age, which covered almost one third of the earth's surface with glaciers as recently as 18,000 years ago, is also under continuing investigation. For years, people have argued about whether the Ice Age has really come to an end, or whether we are still in the Ice Age and living in a relatively brief cycle when the climate warms, only to cool again.

Certainly, our planet is in a cooling trend now. Temperatures began to drop in the mid-1940s, after the world had enjoyed an increasing warm-up over a period of some 50 years. Before that, the climate had been colder than "normal" for several hundred years, and that period of cold is referred to as the Little Ice Age.

Climate fluctuates so much that there really is no such thing as normal. The best evidence indicates that since the last glacial onset, the climate reached its warmest about 8000 B.C. and has been cooling down since then. But the cooling process has not been a steady one, and its fluctuations seem to have coincided with several great historical events. The warm era some 10,000 years ago probably dried up the Sahara and forced the people of North Africa into the oases of the Nile, where they founded civilizations. Prolonged cold spells may have forced the bar-

barian hordes southwestward out of Central Asia to invade the lands of the Roman Empire. A balmy spell around 1000 A.D. probably enabled the Vikings to discover Iceland, Greenland and North America.

When world temperatures drop as they are doing now, the effects of the cooling climate show up first in the upper latitudes. Scientists have observed, for example, that the average growing season in England is two weeks shorter than it was 30 years ago. Iceland's ports have become choked with drift ice as the average temperature has gone down about 3° F. since the 1940s. Such a small decline seems unimportant, but studies of past glacial periods show that a drop of only a few degrees can trigger the growth of glaciers. In fact, some of today's glaciers have started to grow.

Another strong indicator of increasing cold comes from the opposite end of the world: the temperature of the ocean around Antarctica is halfway to the glacial stage. This affects both the Northern and Southern Hemispheres, because water from Antarctica flows in deep, slow currents through the Atlantic and Pacific Oceans and eventually meets Arctic waters.

A bewildering number of theories have attempted to explain ice ages. One claims that volcanic ash blocks out sunlight and thus encourages the growth of ice sheets. Another links open water at the Arctic with circulation of warm currents and greater precipitation, hence more snow that packs into ice sheets. Yet another argues that a decrease in solar energy triggers glaciation.

The explanation most often accepted is a theory first suggested more than 100 years ago. It was proposed again 50 years ago by the Serbian physicist Milutin Milankovitch, whose name has become identified with it. According to Milankovitch, the onset of an ice age is related to the shape of the earth's orbit around the sun and to the position of the earth's axis.

One axial motion that affects climate, so the theory goes, is the wobble that completes a circle every 20,000 years or so (page 12). Another motion is a gradual change in the tilt of the axis with respect to the path of the earth's orbit around the sun. About every 41,000 years, the tilt swings from 22° to 24.5° and back. Every 96,000 years, the shape of the orbit around the sun changes from nearly circular to oval and back again. All of these movements interact in such a way that for certain periods of time, cool summers and mild winters prevail in the upper latitudes of both hemispheres.

It is precisely this situation that favors the birth of huge, ice-age glaciers. Despite the fact that winters would not be as cold, there would still be snow in the far northern and southern latitudes. Cooler summers would mean that less of this snow would melt each year. Thus there would be a buildup of snow, and as new snow was added, the bottom layers would gradually be compressed into ice.

This is the way glaciers form today. They are, however, still confined to the far north and south and to high mountain regions. In an ice age, glaciers can form much farther from the polar regions, and can grow to be so enormous that they engulf even the highest peaks. During the last major glaciation, ice sheets reached as far south as St. Louis, Missouri, in the United States and covered much of Europe. In some areas the glaciers reached a thickness of a mile or more.

Many glacial advances occurred during the Ice Age, which began about one million years ago and is better known as the Pleistocene epoch. Scientists are trying to learn more about the whole history of the Ice Age, and they have discovered that the most detailed record of changes in the climate lies in the sediments of ocean basins.

Thousands of cores of layered sediment have been analyzed following a technique developed by Nobel Laureate Harold Urey to measure certain kinds of oxygen atoms in tiny fossil shells. With this technique, Urey and many others have determined the temperature of water when the sea creatures lived. Then, by measuring radioactivity and magnetism, they have been able to date layer upon layer of shells. Studies show that ocean temperatures have varied by about 10° F. in a 40,000-year cycle, supporting one feature of Milankovitch's theory.

The most convincing support for the theory is based on scores of sediment cores from the Indian Ocean. They contain alternating layers of microfossils that furnish an uninterrupted record extending back 450,000 years.

Some of the organisms liked warm waters, others preferred cold. To study the record of these organisms as fully as possible, an American and British team headed by Columbia University geologist James D. Hays drilled cores that revealed cycles of various time periods. The longest was a span of 93,000 years; another cycle covered 41,000 years. In each case, the microfossils registered changes in the climate that matched those explained by Milankovitch.

Dr. Hays and his group, which includes Dr. Nicholas J. Shackelton of Cambridge University, believe the matching of cores with the earth's motions in space is a positive test of the Milankovitch theory.

Valuable as this is, it does not, however, explain why ice ages first began. The movement of the earth's plates may. Perhaps in the far distant past the continents were arranged so that the North and South Poles were in the middle of large bodies of water. As long as the Poles were at sea, their ice packs must have been held in check by the warmth of the ocean. But when Antarctica, Canada, Siberia and Greenland turned frosty white, and thus reflected more sunlight, the earth must have taken in less of the sun's heat every year. Furthermore, land now blocked the currents of warm water from reaching polar areas. The whole earth, oceans included, must have grown colder.

When the oceans were no longer able to supply enough heat to counteract the trends on land, the glaciers were free to advance and retreat in response to the Milankovitch

The Death of the Sun

SHINING NORMALLY, the sun is seen above the earth at the strength it has had for 5 billion years and will have for 5 billion more. After that, scientists believe, it will heat up and burn out.

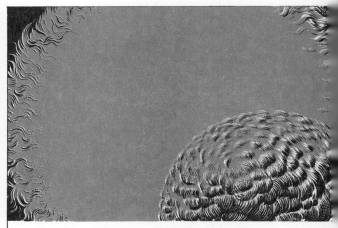

HELIUM forming at the sun's core will gradually expand. It will transform the sun into a type of star called a "red giant," giving off so much heat that the earth's oceans will turn to steam.

cycle. In all likelihood the glaciers will come again many times, to plague human beings and all other living things. It seems that major warm and cold swings can announce themselves fairly abruptly.

If glaciers do grind slowly south again over the next ten to twenty thousand years, either man will have to migrate into the tropics and desert zones of the earth, or he will have to spend considerable power and ingenuity altering the climate in such a way that the advance is halted. If, on the other hand, the earth heats up again, the ice ages will come to an end. The tremendous volume of water locked in the icecaps of Greenland and Antarctica will melt, raising the level of the oceans perhaps 100 feet or more over a long period of time. In this event too man will have to either move or expend enormous

energy and intellect. He will have to either abandon his present coastlands and great port cities or rebuild them, using land fill and dikes extending for many miles.

Modern man, by his very existence, may help bring these rising seas about. Over the last 100 years, factory chimneys have poured a billion tons of carbon dioxide into the atmosphere, increasing its carbon dioxide content by about 10 per cent. By 2000 A.D. a trillion tons of it may have been added.

Since carbon dioxide allows the sun's energy to enter the atmosphere but does not allow it to escape into space, many people argue that this change in the air's content may raise the earth's temperature. In other words, the earth may warm up again, instead of continuing its cooling trend.

SHRINKING AGAIN, after about two billion years as a red giant, the sun will return to its present size above a scorched earth. But it will be dying, and its brightness will be fading.

NEAR DEATH, the sun will be a "white dwarf," about 15 billion years from now. Its fires almost extinguished, it will give off so little heat that the earth will become a dark and frozen mass.

But the labors the earth may require of the human race during future floods or glaciations will be nothing compared to the challenges from outside the earth. The first threat will come from the moon. The tides it raises in the land, sea and air are gradually slowing down the earth's spin. At present the rotation period is lengthening at the rate of about 25 billionths of a second each day. This seems very small, but after five billion years it will give the earth roughly a 36-hour day. Man and his crops should be able to adjust themselves to the warmer 18-hour days and to the equally long, colder nights.

The earth's slowing rotation will be accompanied by a second phenomenon: the moon will begin to move into a larger orbit. It will spiral outward from the earth and it will appear to shine more faintly in the sky. At present the moon is departing from the earth at the rate of about one foot every 30 years.

The gravitational pull of the sun also affects the earth. The sun has always been working with the moon to slow the earth's rotation, and it will continue to do so. At one time, about 375 million years ago, the earth had a 400-day year. This was not because it took the planet any longer to travel around the sun than it now does, but because the days were shorter—slightly less than 22 hours long.

Some time in the future—perhaps in five billion years or so—the sun and moon will have slowed our planet's spin so that a day is 720 hours long—as long as a month. The

(*Text continued on page 122*)

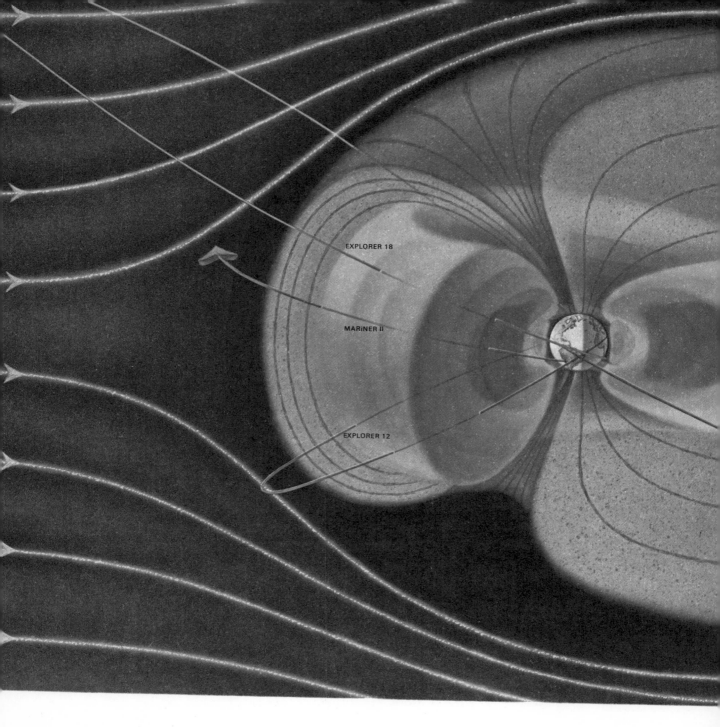

EXPLORER 18

MARINER II

EXPLORER 12

A Cloak of Radiation

Surrounding the earth are several vast layers of
radiation particles trapped in the earth's magnetic
field. These layers were detected by the first
American satellite, Explorer I, and others since then
have yielded more information. (The satellites' paths
are shown in red.) The layers are called the Van

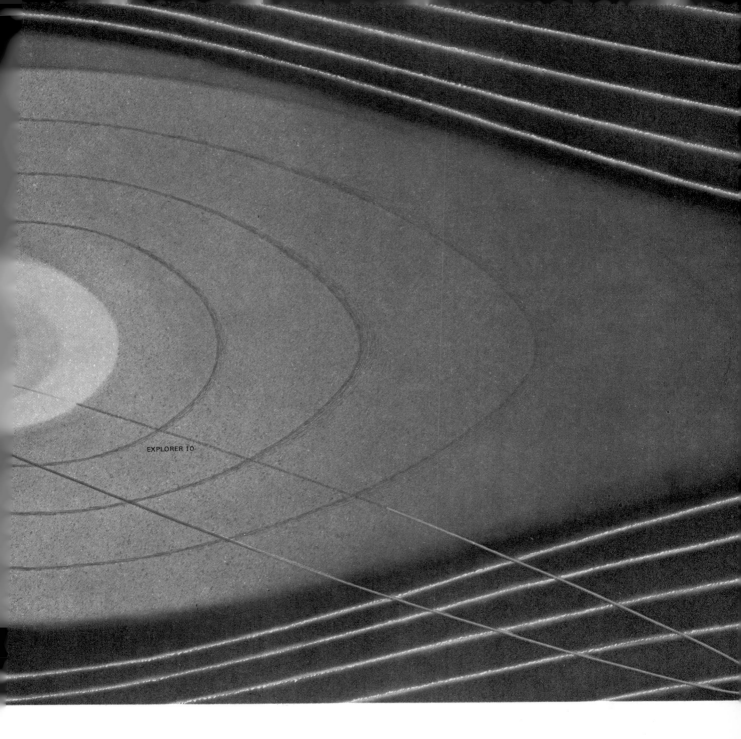

EXPLORER 10

Allen belts, after Dr. James Van Allen, who
identified them. They extend 50,000 miles toward
the sun (*left*) and, buffeted by the solar wind, a
stream of radioactive particles constantly given off
by the sun (yellow lines), they trail off on the
other side of the earth. There are two main kinds
of particles in the belt: negative particles, or
electrons (shown in blue), and positive particles, or
protons (pink and orange). Without these belts, life
on earth, as we know it, would probably not be
able to exist. The belts shield the earth from much
of the lethal radioactivity given off by the sun.

moon now rotates once on its axis as it makes one complete revolution around the earth, and thus always keeps the same face toward us. When the rotation of the earth has been sufficiently slowed, it will always present the same face to the moon. By the time this happens the moon will be nearly half again as far from the earth as it is today.

Astronomers know exactly how the sun will evolve because they have studied sun-like stars that are older than the sun, and have seen how they behave as they begin to run out of the nuclear fuel that makes them burn. When a star of the sun's mass has converted 15 per cent of its original hydrogen into helium, the helium ash that has formed at its core lights up in a second nuclear reaction that is far hotter. As a result the star begins to pour out energy at an increasing rate, swelling and turning blood-red in the process.

About five or six billion years from now the sun will bloat up from its present size until it almost touches its innermost planet, Mercury. At the height of its power, the sun's outpouring of energy will raise the temperature of the earth to about 1,000° F. —a heat so intense that the oceans will turn to steam, and sulphur will boil on the earth's surface.

After the deadly climax of its life, the sun will gradually shrink again and this steaming atmosphere will condense into water once more, flooding the earth. For a few hundred million years the sun will burn with a blue light as it converts the last of its nuclear fuels into metallic elements. During the course of its old age it may undergo eruptions in its outer layers, eruptions that will lay bare its blazing interior and will expose the earth to devastating doses of X-rays and gamma rays.

Finally, the sun will use up the last of its nuclear energy. The waters of the earth will then freeze into a permanent mantle of ice. As the sun cools further, it will continue to shrink under its own weight and will glow feebly for a long, long time. At last, after a lifetime of about 60 billion years, the sun, now completely dark, will course onward through space only as the black corpse of a star, shrunken to incredible density and taking up no more room than a planet. In its final state it will actually be smaller than the earth, but its dense mass will still keep the earth locked in orbit around it.

While the sun is dying, the days on earth will have grown even longer than a month, and the behavior of the moon will begin to change. It will cease its outward spiral and start its long journey back toward the earth; each orbit will be slightly smaller than the last. The moon will regain its present orbit, some 240,000 miles from earth, and continue to grow nearer. But in all likelihood it will not collide with the earth. It may come close enough—within 9,000 miles—to shatter, to be torn apart by the force of the earth's strong gravitational pull. The moon fragments will eventually distribute themselves evenly in a belt that will circle above the earth's equator.

If there are still humans on the planet in that far-off time, they will see not one moon, but tens of thousands of tiny moonlets. From outer space, the earth will closely resemble those other ringed planets of our solar system, Saturn and Neptune.

But today's theorists are beginning to doubt that the sun will remain hot enough long enough for this to happen. They suggest that the sun may go through its final phases too quickly for the earth to have a chance to bring the moon within shattering distance. Instead, the moon's tidal effects may take over again and the moon may once more pull away from the earth. As it drifts off it will have little light to reflect from a dim and dying sun, and the nights will become darker and darker until the moon is no longer visible at all.

Scientists assume that the human race will not live long enough to suffer in the fiery swelling of the sun or the dark doom of the moon. The average life of any one animal species is only about five million years—five million years compared to five billion years before the sun even begins to swell. Even though man will probably fare no better than other animals, there is just a chance that he might. Some kinds of animals have survived unchanged on earth for hundreds of millions of years. What is more, the human species is not subject to the same laws of evolution that have operated up to now. Already man so dominates his planet that the natural evolution of most land plants and large animals has been drastically altered. Man's own evolution has also escaped from the natural channels.

Most scientists take a gloomy view of man's ability to survive his own warlike nature. Yet if the human race does outlive its murderous instincts, it may well plan to outlive the sun as well. Colonizing other planets around stars burning more slowly than the sun may possibly provide a temporary escape for a few fortunate astronauts. The rest of the earth's inhabitants, however, would have to devise a different kind of escape.

At its worst, the sun might scald the earth with heat and cosmic rays so deadly that men could not invent shields against them. It may be that when the heat-death approaches on earth some five billion years from now, human beings will already have moved underground, taking with them as much of the earth's air and water as possible and coating the outsides of their shelters with mirrors to reflect the sun's scorching heat. As the sun cools down, man may find it possible to come out of his artificial caves into the open again and once more devise a new kind of life.

Of course this is all speculation. No one can see that far into the future. But science has found no reason for man's not being able to extend his evolution almost indefinitely—if only he can learn to use his intelligence for his own best ends.

Is Anyone Talking out There?

Shown in a star-streaked time-exposure, the antenna
of a big radio telescope in West Virginia *(left)* listens
for radio signals from space. Shown above is the
control room of the largest radio telescope at the
space research station at Jodrell Bank in England.
Such telescopes have detected mysterious pulsing
radio signals, called pulsars, coming from several
parts of our galaxy. One day they may locate and
identify signals from other intelligent forms of life.

INDEX

Numerals in italics indicate a photograph
or painting of the subject listed.

Air pollution, *48-49*
Aleutians, 95
Allosaurus, 110
Alluvial fans, *89*
Amino acids, 101
Amphibians, 108; lack warmbloodedness, 110
Antarctica, 115, 119
Arctic, 116
Argon, 45, 100
Ascension (island), 80
Asteroids, 22
Asthenosphere, *28-29*, 35, 81, 91, 94, 96
Atmosphere: its composition, 44; its effects, 43-44; parts of, 44-45; pressure of, 44; sucking up of water by, 60, 66; use of radiation by, *44-45*, 46; winds, 45-60
Azores, 80

Badlands, S. Dak., *62-63*
Barnard Glacier, Alaska, *70*
Batholiths, *86-87*, 93-94
Birds: first appearance of, 110; warmbloodedness an asset to, 110
Bora winds, 56
Bryce Canyon, *64*, 67

Cambrian period: extent of ocean in, *102*, 103; life during, 103-104
Cape Cod, Mass., *58-59*, 74
Carbon dioxide, 44, 45; atmospheric, made by man, 119
Carbon-14, as a measure of archeological and geological age, 99, *100*, 101
Carboniferous period: extent of ocean in, *102*, life during, 106-108
Carlsbad Caverns, N. Mex., *68*, 74
Caves, formation of, 69, 74
Cenozoic era, 103; dominance of warmblooded animals since, 110
Clouds, *42-43*, 44, *50-51*, 52, 60; in weather fronts, *46-47*, 51, 52
Coal, 76, *89*, 91; origination of, during Carboniferous period, 108
Colorado Plateau, 67, 69
Colorado River, *23*, 69, 105
Continental drift, *82*, *83*; theory of, 91-94
Continental shelves, 79-80
Continents: floating, 91; glacial scars on southern, 91; movement of, *81*, *82*, 91; as plateaus of rock, 79; roots of, 88; size of, 79-80; theories of origin of, 91-96; thickness of, 88
Cryptozoic eon, 103; few fossil traces, 103
Cyclones, *48-49*, 56

Deserts, early appearance of, 108
Devonian period: extent of ocean in, *102*; life during, 106
Diamonds, *94-95*
Diastrophism, *64-65*, 67, 76, *84*
Dikes, *86-87*, 91

Dinosaurs, age of, 108-110
Draco (constellation), 14

Earth: ancient ideas of, *8-9*; appearance of, from space, *6*, 11-13; as center of universe, 8-9; as target of radiation, *44-45*, *120-121*, 122; asthenosphere, *28-29*, 35, 81, 94, 96, atmospheric levels of, *29*; changing seasons of, 13, *14-15*, 117; continuous motion of, in space, 13-14, internal, *81*; core of, *29*, 35-36; cross section of, *29*; crust of, *29*, 31, 33, 34, 36, *39*, 75, 76, 80, *81*, 85-86, 88, 94, 95, 96, 116; early theories of origin of, 25-26; evolution of life on, *104-105*; first dimensions of, 9-10; frozen future of, *112*, *118-119*; and growth of glaciers, 116-118; incorrectly known local curvature of, 114-115; lithosphere, *28-29*, 31, 35, 81, 94, 96; magnetic field of, 36-40; magnetic poles of, 36-38, 91-94; mantle of, *29*, 35, *81*; most of, under water, 79; origin of, 22, *24-25*, 26-28; rotation of, and winds, 46-49, 56; shifting axis of, *12*, 13, *14-15*, 117; slowing rotation of, 119, 122; temperature of core of, 28; weighing of, 28-31
Earth scientists, work of, 114-115
Earthquakes, *37*; Calabria, Italy, *33*; frequency of, 31; Guatemala, 32; inadequate knowledge of, 33-34; Lisbon, 32, 33; San Andreas fault, 31, 32, *41*, 96; San Francisco, 32; shock waves from, 33, *34-35*, 36, *37*; zones of, 31, *32-33*, 88
Eratosthenes, 9-10
Erosion, *64-76*; by glaciers, *70-71*, *89*; by Mississippi River system, 66; by the oceans, 59, 74, *77*; down-cutting, 69; effects of water, *23*, *64-65*, 66-69, 71, *72-73*, *74-75*; formation of Grand and Bryce canyons, *23*, 67, 69; in desert areas, 71-73; of Badlands, S. Dak., *62-63*; side-cutting, 69, *74-75*; through rock layers, *23*, 67, 69; underground, *68-69*, 73-74
Evolution, 101, 110; picturization of, *104-105*
Exosphere, 44, 45

Faults, 31-32, *41*, 81
Fish, evolution of, 104, 106, *110*; fossil, *111*
Flood plains, 66-69
Fossils: dating of by carbon-14, *100*, *101*; dinosaur, 98; found in sedimentary rocks, 80, *105*, *107*, *111*, 117; of ancient bacteria, *109*; study of, *38*, 40
Fronts, weather, *46-47*, 51-52
Fumaroles, *30*

Geologists, 63, 64, 91, 96, 99-100, 103
Gilbert, William, 36
Glaciers, *70-71*, *89*; depressing of

Scandinavia by, 88; development of, during Permian period, 108; factors increasing growth of, 117-118; next coming of, and world changes, 115-119; traces of, on southern continents, 91
Grand Canyon, *23*, 67, *105*
Greenland, 100, 119
Guatemala, 32
Gypsum, 76, *89*

Hawaiian Islands, growth of, 85
Hays, James D., 117
Helium, 45, 118, 122
Himalayas, 96
Hot spot, 88, 96
Hurricanes, 56, *57*, 58, 60
Hydrogen, 45, 122

Ice Age(s), 115-119
Iceland, 115
India, 96
Insects: development of, 108; lack warmbloodedness, 110
International Geophysical Year, 10
Ionosphere, 44, 45

Kilauea (volcano), *27*
Kurile Islands, 95

Labrador, 100
Laccoliths, *86-87*
Land bridges, possible growth of new, 116
Lava, 27
Lightning, *52-53*
Lisbon earthquake, 32
Lithosphere, *28-29*, 31, 35
Luray Cave, Va., 74

Magma, 86
Magnetic compass, 36, 38, 40
Magnetic field (earth's): protection from radiation by, 38-40; reversals of, 36, 38-40, 91-94; source of, 36
Mammals: first appearance of, 110; warmbloodedness an asset to, 110
Mammoth Cave, Ky., 74
Man: may cause rise in oceans, 119; possible end of, 113, *123*; problems for, with next ice age, 118-119; surviving the holocaust, 122-123
Mantle, *28-29*, 81
Marian Islands, 95
Mene rhombeus (ancient fish), *111*
Mesosphere, 44, 45
Mesozoic era, 103; dominance of reptiles in, 108-110
Meteorites: composition of, 20, 22, 36; effect of, on earth, 17, *20-21*; estimated age of, 100-101; and moon, 16, 17, *18-19*, 22
Meteoroids, 20
Meteorologists, 44
Meteors, 20, 22, 36, 40, 100

Michell, John, 33
Mid-Atlantic Ridge, 80, 88
Mid-ocean ridge, 81
Milankovitch, Milutin, 117
Milky Way, 7, *10-11*, 14
Miller, Dr. Stanley, *109*
Minerals: Amethyst, *92;* Azurite, *92;*
    Chalcanthite, *92;* Chrysotile, *92;*
    Diamond, *94-95;* Garnet, *92;* Limonite,
    92; Malachite, *92;* Microcline, *93;*
    Pyrite, *92;* Quartz, *92;* Ruby sphalerite,
    93; Smoky quartz, *93;* Variscite, *92;*
    Yellow carnotite, *97;* Yellow wulfenite,
    93. See also Rocks
Mississippi River, 66, 75
Mistral winds, 56
Monsoon winds, 54-56
Moon, 8, 14-20; attraction of, *38;*
    Copernicus crater on, *18-19;* craters on,
    16, 17; earth's rotation slowed by,
    119-121; effect of meteorites on, *18-19;* in
    50 billion years, *112;* possible future of,
    114-115; "seas" on, 16, 17; surface of, by
    "earthshine," *16-17*
Moraines, *70,* 89
Mountains: disappearance of, *78;*
    floating, 88-91; formation of, during
    Carboniferous period, 106; formation
    of by warping, *84;* by plate movement,
    95-96; intensive building of, during
    Permian, 108

Neptunists, 86
New Zealand, 95
Newton, Isaac, 10, 114
Nile River, 118
Nitrogen, 44, 45
North Star. *See* Polaris, *12,* 14, 36
Nyamlagira (volcano), *26*

Oceans: ancient, as source of life, 110;
    annual drop in levels of, 114; as
    depositories of river sediments, 74-76; as
    erosive forces, *58-59,* 74, *76-77;* basins
    of, 80; end of the, 118, 122; extent of
    during geological periods, *102;* floor
    of, 80; Ice Age end to raise level of, 119;
    man may cause rising of, 119; Project
    Mohole under, 36; temperature
    variations of, in Ice Age, 116-118
Ordovician period: extent of ocean in, *102,*
    104; life during, 104
Oxygen, 43, 44, 45, 83
Ozone, 44, 45

Pacific "ring of fire." *See* Earthquakes,
    zones of
Palaeontologists, *38*
Palaeozoic era, 103
Pamlico Terrace, S.C., *78*
Pangaea, 88, 96
Permian period, changes during, 108
Phanerozoic eon, 103; three subdivisions

(eras) of, 103
Plates: 31, 79; action of, 81, 88, 94-96;
    earthquakes and, 31, 88; number of,
    94; volcanoes and, 94
Plutonists, 86
Polaris, *12,* 14, 36
Precipitation, *42-43,* 60, 66; in changing
    weather fronts, *46-47*
Pulsars, 124

Radiation: as power source, *44-45,* 46;
    effects of, 38-40; protection by ozone
    against, 44, 45; Van Allen belts, *120-121*
Radio telescope, *124-125*
Radioactive carbon. *See* Carbon-14
Radioactive dating, 99, *100,* 101
Rainbows, *61*
Reptiles, development of, 108;
    dominance of, in Mesozoic era, 108-110;
    flying, 110; lack warmbloodedness, 110
River deltas, 74-75
Rivers, aging of, 66-69
Rock slumps, 89
Rock: basalt, 80, 85, 86, *87,* 88, 96;
    batholiths, 85, *86-87;* bituminous
    (soft) coal, *89;* breaks in crustal, cause
    earthquakes, 31-32; breccia, *89;*
    components of, 83; in earth's crust, 80;
    conglomerate, 75, *89;* coquina, *89;*
    Cryptozoic, 103; cutting of, by rivers, *23,*
    67, 69, 72-73; and diastrophism, 64-
    65, *84;* dikes, 85, *86-87;* diorite, *86;*
    dolomite, 80; gabbro, *87;* gneiss, *90;*
    granite, *65,* 73, 80, 85, 86, 88, *90,* 96, 100;
    gypsum, *89;* hornfels, *90;* igneous, 75,
    80, *86-87;* in glaciers, *70-71;* in volcanoes,
    26-27, 83; iron-bearing, indicating
    shift in magnetic field, 38, 91-94;
    laccoliths, *86-87;* lava, 27, 83-85;
    limestone, *64, 68-69,* 74, 75, 76, 80, 83, 89-
    90; magma, 83-85, *86-87,* 95, 96;
    marble, 83, *90;* metamorphic, 80-83, 86,
    90; obsidian, 85, *86;* phyllite, *90;*
    pumice, *86;* quartzite, 83, *90;* rhyolite, *87;*
    sandstone, 75, 80, *89, 90;* schist, *90;*
    sedimentary, 80, *84, 86, 89, 105;*
    sedimentary, creation of, 74-76, 84,
    86, *89;* shale, 75-76, 80, *89, 90;* sills, 85,
    86-87; slate, 80, *90;* three basic groups
    of, 80; travertine, *89;* tuff, *87;* volcanic,
    64, 80, 83; weathering of, *64-65,* 73-74,
    77. *See also* Minerals

Salt, deposits of, 76, 104-106, 108
San Andreas fault, 31-32, *41,* 96
San Francisco earthquake, 32, 40
Saturn (planet), 31, 115
Scandinavia, rising of, 88
Scorpions, *105,* 106
Seismic waves, 33, *34,* 35
Seismologists, 31, 35
Shields, 103
Sills, *86-87,* 91

Silurian period: life during, 106; salt
    deposits of, 104-106
Sink-holes, 74
Sirocco (winds), 56
Smaze, *48-49*
Solar system, 7, 19, 100; origin of, 26-28;
    unusual orbits in, 28
Solar wind, *120-121*
Squall line, 52
Stegosaurus, 108-110
Story of Mankind, The, 101
Strain meter, *39*
Stratosphere, 44, 45
Sun, 7, *10-11,* 13, 14; extinction of, *112,*
    118-119; radiation of, as energy source,
    44-45, 46, 49, 116; theories of origins
    of, *26-28*

Temperature: cycle of, in ice-ages, 115-118;
    historical significance of fluctuations
    in, 118; period of warmest, 118
Temple of Serapis, 64
Tibetan Plateau, 96
Tides, 114, 119
Tornadoes, 52-54; damage from, *55*
Trenches, 80, *81,* 94-96
Trilobites, 104, 106, 108
Tristan da Cunha (island), 80
Troposphere, 44, 45
Typhoons. *See* Hurricanes
Tyrannosaurus, 110

Unconformities, 76
Uranium: prospecting for, *97;* value of,
    to geologists, 100
Uranus, 28
Urey, Harold, 116, 117

Van Allen, Dr. James, *120-121*
Van Loon, Hendrik, 101
Vega, *12,* 14
Venus, 28
Vikings, explorations of, 90
Volcanoes, *26-27,* 60, 81, 83-85, *86-87;*
    activity of, during Carboniferous period,
    106; shield, *86-87*

Warmbloodedness, advantages of, 100
Water: erosive effects of, *64-65,* 66-69, 71,
    72-73, 74-75, 76-77; in strong winds,
    56-58; in the atmosphere, 45, 60, 66; in
    waterspouts, 54; on the young earth,
    24-25; rock-cutting by, *23, 67,* 69;
    underground, *30, 68-69,* 73-74
Water cycle, *30,* 60, 66
Waterspouts. *See* Tornadoes
Weather. *See* Fronts
Weathering. *See* Erosion
Wegener, Alfred, 91, 94
Winds, 46-60

Yellow River, 66
Yellowstone River, *74*

Credits

The sources for the illustrations that appear in this book are shown below. Credits for the pictures from left to right are separated by commas, from top to bottom by dashes.

Cover—Juan Guzman
Table of Contents—Joseph Bertelli—Adolph E. Brotman—Dan Todd—Matt Greene—Lowell Hess—Adolph E. Brotman—Axel Ebel
6—NASA
8, 9—Joseph Bertelli
10-11—Antonio Petruccelli
12—Matt Greene
14-15—Joseph M. Secacca courtesy American Museum of Natural History—Ralph Crane from Black Star, Hugh Morton from Alpha Photo Associates, Inc.
16-17—Mel Hunter
18-19—Lick Observatory Photo, NASA—NASA
20-21—Jack Birns—J. R. Eyerman
23—Frank J. Scherschel
24-25—Gordon Parks
26, 27—Eliot Elisofon, Camera Hawaii from Alpha Photo Associates, Inc.
29—David Klein
30—Brian Brake from Magnum
32-33—Courtesy International Seismological Survey
34, 35—Adolph E. Brotman

37—Carnegie Institute of Washington—Carl Mydans
38, 39—Fritz Goro, J. R. Eyerman
41—Fairchild Aerial Surveys, Inc.
42-43—Eliot Elisofon
44, 45—Nicholas Fasciano
46-47—Dan Todd
48-49—Eric Schaal, Victor H. Waldrop
50-51—Royal Meteorological Society except centre top Jesse Lunger from Black Star
52-53—Ted Bank from Monkmeyer Press Photos, Horace S. Benson courtesy General Electric Corp., Yitka Kilian, U.S. Naval Ordnance Laboratory
54, 55—Bill Burkett, George Yates for *The Des Moines Register*.
57—Weather Bureau Miami, Florida, courtesy NASA
58-59—Daniel Farber from Rapho Guillumette
61—Richard Jepperson from Alpha Photos
62-63—Grant Heilman
64-65—Emil Schulthess from Black Star, Josef Muench

(2), Douglas P. Wilson, Robert Walsh, Emil Schulthess from Black Star
67—Nino Carbe
68, 69—Josef Muench, art by Matt Greene
70, 71—Bradford Washburn, William M. Lee
72, 73—Ray Atkeson
74, 75—Andreas Feininger, Nicholas Fasciano courtesy Dr. Luna B. Leopold
76, 77—N. R. Farbman
78—Walter Dawn
81, 82—David Klein
84—R. H. Chapman U.S. Geological Survey
86, 87—Lee Boltin except drawing Lowell Hess
89—Lee Boltin except drawing Lowell Hess
90—Lee Boltin (3)—Paul Jensen, Lee Boltin (2)—Paul Jensen (2), Lee Boltin—drawing by Lowell Hess
92—Dmitri Kessel, courtesy American Museum of Natural History—Dmitri Kessel (2)—courtesy American Museum of Natural History, Dmitri Kessel
93—Dmitri Kessel, Russ

Kinne from Photo Researchers Inc.—courtesy American Museum of Natural History, Dmitri Kessel—Floyd R. Getsinger, courtesy American Museum of Natural History
94, 95—Bob Landry, Lee Boltin, Margaret Bourke-White
97—George Silk
98—National Park Service
100-102—Adolph E. Brotman
104—Adolph E. Brotman
105—Antonio Petruccelli
107—top left Mark A. Binn, top right (2) Carroll Lane and Mildred Adams Fenton—courtesy F. M. Carpenter
109—William Schopf and Elso S. Barghoorn—U.P.I.— William Schopf and Elso S. Barghoorn
111—Carroll Lane and Mildred Adams Fenton
112—Mel Hunter
114, 115—Alex Ebel
118, 119—Alex Ebel
122, 123—Andreas Feininger, Larry Burrows
End papers—Gloria Cernosia

For Further Reading

Ames, Gerald, and Rose Wyler, *Planet Earth*. Golden, 1963.
Asimov, Isaac, *The Double Planet* (rev. ed.). Abelard-Schuman Ltd., 1967.
Branley, Franklyn M., *Book of Planet Earth for You*. Crowell, 1975.
Earth: Planet Number Three. Crowell, 1966.
Chandler, M. H., *Man's Home: The Earth*. Rand McNally and Co., 1965.

Creative Editors, *History of the Earth*. Creative Educational Society, 1971.
Dwiggins, Don, *Spaceship Earth: A Space Look at Our Troubled Planet*. Childrens, 1970.
Fodor, R. V., *Meteorites: Stones from the Sky*. Dodd, Mead, 1976.
Heller, Robert et al., *Challenges to Science: Earth Science*. McGraw-Hill, 1973.

Honolka, Kurt, *To Prove the Earth Is Round, the Story of Magellan*. Astor-Honor, 1969.
Mathews, William H., 3rd, *Story of the Earth*. Harvey, 1968.
Paradis, Adrian A., *Reclaiming the Earth*. David Mckay, 1971.
Pilkington, Roger, *The River*. H. Z. Walck, Inc., 1963.
Rosenfeld, Sam, *Ask Me a*

Question About the Earth. Harvey, 1966.
Shannon, Terry, and Charles Payzant, *Project Sealab: The Story of the United States Navy's Man-In-The-Sea Program*. Golden Gate Junior Books, 1966.
Spar, Jerome, in cooperation with the American Museum of Natural History, *The Way of the Weather*. Creative Educational Society, 1962.

Acknowledgments

The editors are indebted to Dr. Wallace S. Broecker, Professor of Geology, Columbia University, New York City, New York, who read and commented on the entire text. The editors are also indebted to the staff of the LIFE Nature Library edition of *The Earth*, from which this volume has been adapted. The staff for this edition was Ogden Tanner, editor; Eric Gluckman, designer; Jonathan Kastner, Marianna Kastner, writers; Eleanor Feltser, Susan Marcus, Theo Pascal, Kelly Tasker, researchers; Grace Fitzgerald, copyreader; Gloria Cernosia, art assistant.